"This basic primer for parents is a helpful guideline into the different parenting styles and their effects on children. The book is a welcome, common sense approach for parents who want to build healthy relationships with their children based on mutual love and respect. I particularly like the way the chapters are laid out with main ideas, examples and practical exercises. Parents and educators will find, Your Living Legacy, a meaningful text to consider as a tool in parenting."

--Professor Sally Nalven, Child Development Department
San Diego Miramar College

"Parenthood is often considered instinctive, yet it remains mankind's hardest task. It is a fine art in need of both education and practice. Your Living Legacy, by Dr. Shelli Chosak clarifies some of the points other books may have left ambiguous. Years of experience give the author a unique opportunity to re-examine this time-old subject. As a mother of three grown children, and one who had proudly considered herself 'good,' I learned much from it. May these guidelines give younger parents the tools to avoid some of the mistakes many of us have made along the way."

--Zohreh Ghahremani, Author of _The Moon Daughter_

"As a family law attorney in practice for 43 years, I recognized a lot of the issues and solutions to parenting problems in Dr. Chosak's book that I encounter in my everyday family law/custody practice. I would highly recommend this book to any mother with young children. Raising children is the most difficult job anyone can do. How well one recognizes the positive and the negative parenting influences to which they have been subjected as children, and which they want to emulate, avoid, or modify will make a huge difference in how their own children, especially daughters will adapt in their lives. Read this book, and apply the lessons that you learn—your children will thank you for it."

--Alexandra Leichter, Certified Family Law Attorney

YOUR LIVING LEGACY

How Your Parenting Style
Shapes the Future for You and Your Child

First Edition Design Publishing

DEDICATION

This book could never have been written without the unwavering support of my three children, Mark, Jodi, and Jamie. They have provided inspiration, encouragement, and valuable feedback. They have given me an education I could not have acquired in any other meaningful way.

To my late father, Jack Berke, who was one of the best role models of positive parenting I have known.

To my dear friend and colleague, Gloria Richfield, Ph.D. She encouraged the birth of this book after attending one of the Mother/Daughter workshops I conducted. We collaborated on the writing for several months, and she was a constant source of loving support and wisdom.

TABLE OF CONTENTS

ON CHILDREN

Kahlil Gibran

Your children are not your children
They are the sons and daughters of Life's longing for itself.
They come through you but not from you,
And though they are with you yet they belong not to you.

You may give them your love but not your thoughts,
For they have their own thoughts.
You may house their bodies but not their souls
For their souls dwell in the house of tomorrow,
which you cannot visit, not even in your dreams.
You may strive to be like them,
but seek not to make them like you.
For life goes not backward nor tarries with yesterday.

You are the bows from which your children
as living arrows are sent forth.
The archer sees the mark upon the path of the infinite,
and He bends you with His might
that His arrows may go swift and far.
Let your bending in the archer's hand be for gladness;
For even as He loves the arrow that flies,
so He loves also the bow that is stable.

The Prophecy, 1923 /Alfred A. Knopf, 1973[1] (with permission)

INTRODUCTION: HOW TO BECOME THE BEST PARENT YOU CAN BE

"Work On Yourself: This is what many of the parenting books ignore -- and it may be the most important." (In a comment posted to the Barking up the Wrong Tree blog by Eric Barker[2] on June 14, 2015)

This is a book about discovery--about *You* as a parent and how you can become the best parent you can be.

Why you should read this book:
- To understand your parenting style and how it impacts your relationship with your child
- To recognize signs of disengagement with your child; take steps to prevent harm; identify words and actions that work.
- To learn more about your child, yourself, and the ways you can enhance the relationship for both of you

Benefits of exploring your parenting style(s):
Understanding your parenting style(s) provides a valuable opportunity for self-reflection and enables you to evaluate:

- The effectiveness of a given style
- The aspects of a given style that are positive for your child and your relationship
- The aspects of a given style that may detract from your child's healthy development
- The style(s) that can be modified or utilized to address particular situations
- How some of the behaviors you observe in your child are consequences of the style you are using
- How your style may assist or interfere with some of the lessons you want to teach your child
- What steps you might want to take to improve your relationship with your child even if she is now an adult

The following questions provide a personal framework or reference point when reading through the styles.

1. How much thought have you given to who has influenced how you parent and in what ways?
2. Have you made a conscious decision to repeat or reject how you were parented?
3. What factors have gone into those choices? For example: Did you personally feel neglected, deprived, nourished, or encouraged by the behaviors of your parents or other caregivers?
4. How successful is your parenting style? How do you measure the results?
5. Have you looked at the effects your parenting style has had on your child, your relationship, and the well-being of each of you?
6. Have you read books or articles, taken classes, or followed advice on how to parent?
7. Have you found information that is helpful? How well has it worked?

As you may have already discovered, the path of parenting is filled with mine fields.

The choices you make, based on the advice you receive, the books you read, or the lessons you learn, do not necessarily translate into the parent you are--or become.

How you parent is influenced by messages you have internalized long ago that can pop up without warning. While you may be a conscious, caring, and responsible parent a good deal of the time, unwanted behaviors often appear when you are under stress.

Or, perhaps you have based your parenting philosophy on being determined to avoid the mistakes your parents made, and end up making the mistakes they avoided.

The biggest challenge is not how closely you can follow any theory or practice that sounds good, but how you can quiet the voices in your head that interrupt or sabotage your best intentions.

PROLOGUE: THE BIRTH OF THIS BOOK

I'm a grandmother now. A central focus of my life has been finding ways to create quality relationships through continual study and as a licensed psychotherapist, working with parenting and mother/daughter relationships for many years. I am the mother of a son and two daughters, and a grandmother of four boys and one girl. Fortunately, my children have somehow made it to adulthood without any major scars, though there are minor ones. I prefer to look at "scars" as learning lesions, similar to the wrinkles we acquire as we age, which reveal our accumulated wisdom. Those scars are inevitable, the effect of being willing to engage in the challenge to grow up as whole and healthy as possible. Some of the scars for my children are the result of losing their father at an early age – they were five, nine, and eleven -- and my often compromised efforts to be a good mother and substitute father figure.

Many of the scars are the consequence of my well-intentioned but insufficient parenting skills, as well as a lack of understanding of what to expect and how to meet and manage the various developmental stages all children experience. There are also the scars my children acquired in their struggle to discover and understand who they are, whether or not it was in agreement with my own notions of how I wanted to see them. I took parenting classes, read books and talked to anyone I thought was wiser than me on the subject. I also studied psychology, earning Bachelor's, Master's and eventually Doctoral degrees. A particularly important aspect of my education was learning from my children. They taught me things I hadn't read in any books or learned in any parenting classes. Today, I can gratefully say I have a very good relationship with all three of my children and five grandchildren. It has come about with great effort and determination, and I have my own battle scars, mostly healed, to show for it.

During my professional career as a therapist and teacher, I was asked to be a speaker at a women's philanthropic group. Since the event was close to Mother's Day, they asked me to speak on the topic of Mothers and Daughters. I was familiar with the group, women in their fifties and sixties, from traditional backgrounds. I knew what I wanted to say and also knew they might not like to hear some of it. Nevertheless, I believed it was valuable information. On the morning of the presentation, the

Program Director called to say, "We normally expect about sixty women, but just found out there is a competing event which means the attendance will more likely be around forty women." When 150 women showed up, we were astounded! It was the subject matter that drew them there, not my stellar reputation as a speaker (I had only done occasional speaking at that point).

After my presentation, the women clamored for more information. "What books could we read? Where could we learn more?" The woman who was the Administrator of a program I was directing suggested we offer a Mother and Daughter workshop. The response was enthusiastic. For the next three years, I conducted four daylong workshops each year, all very well attended—seventy-five to one hundred women came each time. I designed the workshops to be experiential and interactive. Some women showed up with their daughters. At times even three generations attended. Some women came alone, wanting to understand their relationship with their mothers, even if deceased, or because their daughters were unwilling to come. My therapy practice became filled with mothers and daughters wanting to improve or heal their relationships.

This book has been in process for many years and is based on material developed for those workshops. I started writing more than fifteen years ago, and then put it aside as other life and career demands interfered. Now I realize the seasoning and mature reasoning and perspective I've acquired in the intervening years was of great help in creating the finished product.

The Parenting Styles listed in this book are descriptive of the dynamics I observed working with individuals and families during my more than twenty-five years as a psychotherapist and in my coaching practice.

YOUR
LIVING LEGACY

How Your Parenting Style
Shapes the Future for You and Your Child

By

Shelli Chosak, Ph.D.

Chapter 1:

GUIDELINES FOR READING THIS BOOK

As you read this book, keep in mind the following guidelines and assumptions:

1. A sincere desire to improve your relationship with your child/children.
2. A willingness—and open mind to explore your intended and current parenting practices.
3. Objectivity—read from an observer's stance. This requires you to take a step back and engage the left side of your brain: logical vs. your right brain/emotional side.
4. Be able to evaluate your child's inborn temperament and inclinations without bias, and adjust or compensate your style to reflect their individual characteristics.
   (Premise: We are born with an inclination towards a given temperament. This will be modified by our environment, either positively or negatively. Our "environment" includes parenting influences, siblings and extended family, teachers, spiritual leaders, and friends.)
5. Recognize while some parenting styles may appear wholly negative or positive, no one style is all constructive or detrimental. Much depends on how it is used and to what extent.
6. After each Parenting Style, there is a rating scale. Circle the number that best fits your parent(s), spouse and you a majority of the time.
7. The vignettes included in each style are designed to illustrate more extreme examples of the style to provide a clear perspective from which to evaluate your own level of involvement.
8. "Style" doesn't necessarily mean it's what you *always* do. It may refer to a tendency you have to react in a certain way when you are not being your best self due to stress, anxiety, or other life pressures.
9. Style can also refer to a conscious or sub-conscious decision you've made as to how you want to be as a parent. Your choices

are based on your own experiences growing up and/or what you think will produce the desired outcomes you have for your child.

10. Many parenting books and articles concentrate on the child as "the problem." This book focuses on what the parent is doing that might create or contribute to the problem. *Not all children's issues are your "fault."* To the extent you can alleviate distress or improve on your child's well-being, you will feel more competent and comfortable. However, there are circumstances which, despite your very best skills and efforts, will not be successful due to genetic or other environmental factors. It is also not unusual for your relationship with your spouse to influence your parenting style. The bonus: learning more about yourself will not only benefit your relationships, it will be empowering.

Note: For purposes of simplification, the examples of parents and children are expressed in the female gender. Most of the descriptions will be particularly relevant to the mother/daughter relationship. (The examples are all taken from real life situations. Names and some details have been changed to protect the identity of those portrayed.)

The mother-daughter relationship is often more complex than the mother-son or father-daughter relationships. What complicates the relationship is the seeming paradox of the mother as a role model to her daughter, and the daughter's developmental need to differentiate herself in order to find her own true identity while maintaining a healthy relationship with her mother.

For this reason, the focus on the mother-daughter relationship is likely the most challenging, both from the perspective of the unique issues mothers and daughters confront and because it provides some of the most substantive material for you to learn about yourself.

While this book is mainly written for mothers and daughters, fathers can benefit from the information as well. And much of what is written here can similarly apply to sons.

MOST COMMON THEMES THAT DERAIL US

The following themes can occur when we are under stress: tired, preoccupied, pressured, insecure due to lack of information or confidence in our abilities.

- Loss of control
- Fear of failure
- Fear of success
- Feeling unlovable
- Feeling incompetent-- can't measure up to our own standards or expectations of others
- Perfectionism
- Making inaccurate assumptions and acting on them as if they are true
- Lack of trust in our own personal resources
- Lack of trust in our ability to recover from harm to ourselves or those we care about
- Fear of feeling-- or expressing our own feelings
- Fear of others' feelings --anger, helplessness, sadness or other distress
- Fear of being judged
- Lack of trust in other person
- Trying to figure others out and how we can get what we need or want from others

These activities consume a large amount of physical time and negative mental and emotional energy. A more productive use of our mental efforts is to learn how *we keep ourselves* from having the quality of relationships we want.

Chapter 2:

BACKGROUND: EVOLUTION OF OUR PARENTING STYLES

"Parenting practices are defined as specific behaviors that parents use to socialize their children", while parenting style is "the emotional climate in which parents raise their children."[3]

"A child's temperament and parents' cultural patterns have an influence on the kind of parenting style a child may receive."[4]

A review of the literature on parenting styles yields theories from several prominent professionals in the field. One of the most notable is Diana Baumrind[5], a developmental psychologist who originally identified three basic parenting styles. Many of the theories that followed were based on her model of Authoritarian, Permissive, and Authoritative styles

During the early 1960s, Baumrind conducted a study on more than 100 preschool-age children. Using naturalistic observation, parental interviews and other research methods, she identified four important dimensions of parenting:

- Disciplinary strategies
- Warmth and nurturance
- Communication styles
- Expectations of maturity and control

Researchers have uncovered convincing links between parenting styles and the effects these styles have on children.

Further research by Maccoby and Martin[6] also suggested the addition of a fourth parenting style called Uninvolved Parenting.

"There is no universally 'best' style of parenting," writes author Douglas Bernstein in his book *Essentials of Psychology*. (2011)[7]

In reading Dr. Baumrind's and Dr. Macoby's work, I realize, like so many other aspects of our lives, parenting is influenced by our culture and the times in which we live. Each generation is influenced by previous generations and has its impact on subsequent generations.

For example, children who were raised in the era following The Great Depression were taught to be thrifty, and they were often subject to stricter parenting and encouraged to be self-reliant. As the children raised in that generation became parents and more economically self-sufficient, they wanted to give their children what they didn't have. Many became more indulgent materially and more lenient with their child's behavior.

Another effect of our cultural evolution has been the increased exposure to life outside the immediate family and community. Different eras influence the morality and social norms and modify some of the more traditional parental views and values. As the world becomes more accessible and higher education more available, competition increases and many parents become more inclined to teach their children to be high achievers.

The style of parenting you choose is strongly influenced by how you were raised as a child. You may choose to adopt the same style or a different one, largely dependent on how beneficial you think your parents' methods were. You may choose to reject the style you were raised with yet still repeat it without consciously realizing you are doing so.

Attempting to fit yourself into three or four categories can limit your appreciation of all the intricacies involved in parenting. Expanding the list of styles to twenty will help you more clearly identify your actions, and the impact they have on your relationship with your child and your own well-being.

This book broadens the basic concepts and illustrates how parenting has evolved. It is also designed to fine tune and further illuminate some of the issues involved in the very complex job of effective parenting. Since each of us is unique, an attempt to classify yourself into a narrow number of styles limits exploration of your individuality and influences. It also doesn't take into account the myriad ways you express your beliefs and experiences. If you look at parenting styles in more detail, you may notice aspects of your parenting you haven't thought much about or considered what influence your style might have on your children. In short, it's an opportunity to provide more information on the immensely complicated job of parenting.

Having said that, it is important not to overanalyze yourself or become fixated on aspects of your parenting that may have little or no effect on how your children turn out. As a parent and a human, you are not perfect, and seeking that perfection can create more problems than it solves. In your quest to attain perfection, you will inevitably become irritated and judgmental of yourself, resulting in feelings of frustration, inferiority or inadequacy. This is not a healthy mental state to maximize your abilities as a parent. It is important to recognize there is value and beauty in imperfection, it is so honestly human and real—a much better model for your children.

Chapter 3:

DEVELOPMENTAL INFLUENCES ON PARENTING

In looking at developmental influences, we take into consideration both the influence and effect of our own environment growing up, as well as the environment our children are experiencing.

As infants, we start life off with a purity of innocence that comes with absence of experience as well as an undeveloped brain. In the first months of life, if we receive our basic needs of love, comfort, and cuddling, we will perceive the world as safe and our sense of being as intact.

Next the socialization process necessary for our adaptation to life begins. How we progress is influenced by how we see and value ourselves. We begin to make adjustments in our behaviors to facilitate our survival as we perceive it. The work of Erik Erikson on *Stages of Psychosocial Development* [8] is basic to understanding what we need to learn for the healthy development of our self-concept. (His books also addressed implications on how we decide what kind of parent we will be.)

Erik Erikson's theory of psychosocial development is one of the best-known theories of personality in psychology. His theory describes the impact of social experience across the whole lifespan.

One of the main elements of Erikson's Psychosocial Stage theory is the development of Ego Identity. According to Erikson, Ego Identity is the conscious sense of self we develop through social interaction. He further postulates our Ego Identity is constantly changing due to new experiences and information we acquire in our daily interactions with others. In addition to Ego Identity, Erikson believed a sense of competence also motivates behaviors and actions. Each stage in Erikson's theory is concerned with becoming competent in an area of life. If the stage is managed well, the person will feel a sense of mastery, which he often referred to as ego strength or ego quality. If the stage is managed poorly, the person will emerge with a sense of inadequacy.

In each stage, Erikson believed people experience a conflict that serves as a turning point in development. In Erikson's view, these conflicts are centered on either developing a psychological strength or failing to develop that strength. During these times, the potential for personal growth is high, but so is the potential for failure. The parent plays an important role in the successful progression through stages, especially the earlier ones. For example, in the preschool stage, if the parent allows the child to experiment and explore without undue hovering, criticism or restrictions—within reason—the child will more likely master that stage successfully.

As you go through the sections on Parenting Styles, refer to the following chart. It will help you relate your child's behaviors to her developmental stage and how she might be impacted. It might also be interesting for you to reflect on your own experience growing up and how you moved through each of these stages.

Notes:
1. Erikson's stages are a reflection of the time in which he lived. In today's world, while the stages and their challenges are still relevant, the ages may be somewhat different. For example, in contemporary society, Generativity vs. Stagnation would encompass the years of child-rearing. The self-absorbed mentality of many in our current culture may create a major challenge. It could easily conflict with the need to temporarily abandon one's self-interest for the sake of meeting the developmental needs for the child.
2. Research by Leiner, Marie PhD, and Ataalla, Mohamed MD,[9] on "Mentalization Capacity" refers to the ability to understand behaviors and feelings associated with specific mental states, both in yourself and others. In a general sense, it allows us to recognize the effect that our behavior has on other people, enabling us to be empathetic toward others and to take their perspectives. For various reasons, this capacity may not fully develop in some individuals; as a result, it is difficult for them to understand their own emotions and feelings as well as those of others.

DEVELOPMENTAL STAGES:[10]

Erikson's Stages of Psychosocial Development -- Summary Chart

Stage	Basic Conflict	Important Events	Outcomes
Infancy (birth to 18 months)	Trust vs. Mistrust	Feeding	Children develop a sense of trust when caregivers provide reliability, care, and affection. A lack of this will lead to mistrust.
Early Childhood (2 to 3 years	Autonomy vs. Shame and Doubt	Toilet Training	Children need to develop a sense of personal control over physical skills and a sense of independence. Success leads to feelings of autonomy, failure results in feelings of shame and doubt.
Preschool (3 to 5 years)	Initiative vs. Guilt	Exploration	Children need to begin asserting control and power over the environment. Success in this stage leads to a sense of purpose. Children who try to exert too much power experience disapproval, resulting in a sense of guilt.
School Age (6 to 11 years)	Industry vs. Inferiority	School	Children need to cope with new social and academic demands. Success leads to a sense of competence, while failure results in feelings of inferiority.

Adolescence (12 to 18 years)	Identity vs. Role Confusion	Social Relationships	Teens' needs to develop a sense of self and personal identity. Success leads to an ability to stay true to yourself, while failure leads to role confusion and a weak sense of self.
Young Adulthood (19 to 40 years)	Intimacy vs. Isolation	Relationships	Young adults need to form intimate, loving relationships with other people. Success leads to strong relationships, while failure results in loneliness and isolation
Middle Adulthood (40 to 65 years)	Generativity vs. Stagnation	Work and Parenthood	Adults need to create or nurture things that will outlast them, often by having children or creating a positive change that benefits other people. Success leads to feelings of usefulness and accomplishment, while failure results in shallow involvement in the world, and/or self-absorption
Maturity (65 to death)	Ego Integrity vs. Despair	Reflection on Life	Older adults need to look back on life and feel a sense of fulfillment. Success at this stage leads to feelings of wisdom, while failure results in regret, bitterness, and despair

HIDDEN INFLUENCES:
WHAT KEEPS YOU FROM BEING THE PARENT YOU WANT TO BE

If you are reading this, we can safely assume you care about being the very best parent you can be. You may have read magazine articles, parenting books, and received advice from mothers, grandmothers, friends and others.

And sometimes all that information doesn't produce the results you hope for. It won't always work, even given your best efforts. After all, you are not perfect, you are human. You are subject to the same mood swings, distractions, lack of patience, preoccupations and stresses, as the rest of us.

And sometimes, what keeps you from staying on track and being the parent you want to be, are the hidden influences that seem to surface in spite of your best intentions. Uncovering those influences can illuminate or remove the road blocks that slow or derail your journey to your destination. It requires courage to take a deeper look into the words and actions that sabotage your best efforts.

Eileen was one of those mothers described above: well-educated, responsible and very committed to her parenting skills. She took courses on parenting, read books and articles, and talked to every person she thought was knowledgeable in the area. Her daughter Marni got into a very rough patch as a teenager (a natural and common occurrence), which manifested itself in abusive language directed at her mother. Eileen, while stung, was able to not take it personally. Eileen started practicing everything she thought she had learned, all to no avail.

Eileen paid attention to Marni's claims that she was not listening. Eileen in fact, did not hear what her daughter *attempted* to say. She finally realized what Marni needed was for her mother to *really listen* to her, not on a superficial level, but deep down inside, where her feelings resided. This was a tough call because from Eileen's perspective, Marni regularly exaggerated and even made up accusations about her mother's neglect. Eileen's many attempts to explain or bring out the "truth" did not help. Eileen became determined to find a way to acknowledge Marni on a level meaningful to her daughter.

Eileen realized she needed to dig very deep inside herself, confronting the cherished defenses built up from her own childhood until the present. Her main defenses were denial and innocence, ways of hiding her fears of failure and feelings of inadequacy. What surprised Eileen the most was when she dug deep enough, painful as it was, she would always find *something she could honestly agree with* in Marni's complaints, no matter how minor. Eileen said it was one of the toughest challenges she had to face in her life, and it paid off. Marni was touched by her mother's efforts to really *hear* her, and she was able to calm down and back off. It didn't eliminate all the conflict; that would not have been realistic or even healthy, but it helped forge a deeper and more cooperative relationship between them.

When she was eighteen, Marni presented Eileen with a card on Mother's Day that read: "Mom, you know all the aggravation I've been causing you? Well, I'm almost finished!"

THE EVOLUTION OF OUR PARENTING STYLES

Most parents, whether brand new at the job or seasoned veterans, feel a great sense of responsibility to raise their children to become mentally and physically healthy, productive and successful in their work and personal lives. For some, this desire never leaves, even after their children are grown and on their own. Many believe that parenting is the most important contribution they can make to help create a better world. And, the incredible love they feel for their children inspires desire and determination to make their lives happy and fulfilling.

At odds with the very genuine and altruistic goals of parenting are the ghosts of relationships past, which stir up inevitable human conflicts. No matter how well you were parented, at the heart of your humanness is your ego, and all the subconscious influences that distract you and keep you from acting on your good intentions.

The ego is the hungry child in us. Its' purpose is to feed us emotionally and to devise ways to make us feel better about ourselves. The process is illogical and often random, not achieved by clear thinking and objective information. As a child, when we *accidentally* discover that an action or an event makes us feel more powerful or better about ourselves, we unconsciously integrate this into our psyche as a resource. It is an unsystematic cause and effect sequence of events to which young children attach meaning. We continue the behavior long after we recognize the arbitrary logic. One example: As a young child, you become angry and discover your parent quickly jumps to give you what you want. You've now learned getting angry is a means to get your own way. In another scenario, you become angry and it results in a severe punishment. You've now learned to avoid expressing anger.

You carry these cause and effect relationships into adulthood, and they influence your reactions to other people, most importantly to your children. The following examples are additional illustrations of effects of parental actions on children's behavior:

1. If a child experiences approval for picking up her toys, she learns a way to get rewarded and to feel better.
2. If a child learns manipulating a parent, other adult, or sibling helps her get her way and gives her a sense of control over her environment, she will manipulate to get power.
3. If a child feels physically or emotionally neglected or ignored, she will act out in any way she can to get positive or negative attention. She might start out with a minor test like playing with her food. If she doesn't get the kind of attention she needs, she

will escalate into increasingly stronger behaviors until she finds one or more ways to get a reaction that verifies her presence, her being-ness. Her craving for attention is temporarily satisfied.

All children need attention; it is the means by which they validate their existence. Your view of being-ness and value is initially and primarily achieved by what you read in your parents' eyes (called mirroring). The above examples are only some of the many ways children figure out how to get attention.

If the child is unable to discover satisfactory ways to get positive responses, she will turn to behaviors that result in negative attention. This is preferable to not being noticed at all, even if the negative behaviors result in disapproval or punishment. When she doesn't receive any attention, she will feel invisible, as if she doesn't even exist.

You may recognize some of these examples from your own childhood experiences. How might they affect your own parenting? What effects could they have on your children?

The style of parenting you choose is influenced by your own early development and what tools you have acquired to help you get through life. As you read the descriptions, you may begin to recognize what influences motivated you to adopt the style(s) you have. (See Exercise on Exploring and Understanding Your History at the end of this section.)

There is also a correlation between your parenting style and your child's response. The reactions of your child to the behavior styles you choose can cause you to modify or intensify your actions. It can even cause you to question your regular style and trigger a decision to use a different style. The switch to another style may or may not be an improvement. Examples of your child's reactions are described after each parenting style in the Parenting Styles section.

Daniel Siegel, psychiatrist and author of several excellent books on the developing mind and parenting, addresses the effects of our parenting on our child's brain development. In his book, *Parenting From the Inside Out,* Siegel talks about learning to know yourself as crucial to effective parenting.[11]

When my children were pre-teens, I took my first parenting class, PET or Parent Effectiveness Training.[12] At this point I had my master's degree in psychology, obtained my state license, and established a private practice in marriage and family therapy. I was excited about what I was learning in the PET class and eager to try it out at home. The concepts I learned in the class were not yet fully integrated; I was simply using the principles as "techniques." My efforts met with little success. At one point, my twelve year-old son said to me, "Mom, please don't use that psychology junk on me." I learned a significant lesson in understanding how perceptive our kids can be and how they do know the authentic from the contrived. When I was able to assimilate the information and apply it from an integrated place inside of me, it worked! There were times when a situation came up which called for using the principles I had learned. And, some of those times came when I was tired or not in an objective mood.

I recall saying to myself, "I know what I need to do now, but I just don't feel like it." These were all valuable lessons for me. With all my education, I was still human. You will learn your own lessons (and likely have already learned some). Until you come to understand your own issues, you may not experience and appreciate the effects of your own parenting. It takes considerable self-awareness and time for these lessons to be absorbed and integrated into your own parenting perspectives and practices.

The writing exercise on the next page will give you an opportunity to reflect *before* you read about the Parenting Styles. It provides a starting point to compare your thoughts now, and after you finish reading about the Parenting Styles.

Note:
1. Thomas Gordon[10] began almost forty years ago as the first national parent-training program to teach parents how to communicate more effectively with kids. His goal was to offer step-by-step advice to resolving family conflicts so everybody wins.

EXPLORING AND UNDERSTANDING YOUR HISTORY

Complete this Writing Exercise before you continue to read:

1. Describe the general parenting styles used by your parents:

_____

_____

_____

2. Think about each parent individually and how their styles interacted with each other. How did their styles affect you?

_____

_____

_____

3. If your parents had different styles, describe which one you preferred and why.

_____

_____

_____

4. Were there other parental figures that influenced you growing up? Who were they, and how did their style compare to your parents' style?

_____

_____

_____

5. What choices/decisions did you make about parenting your children as a result of these experiences?

_____

_____

_____

Chapter 4:

MOTHERS AND DAUGHTERS: A UNIQUE RELATIONSHIP

The birth of a daughter can set into motion a complex mixture of feelings: love, tenderness, responsibility, anxiety, even fear. On a logical level, you most likely want your daughter to develop her own identity, to find out who she is as a unique human being apart from being a clone of her mother. This may be incompatible with your emotional longings, setting up myriad internal conflicts that get played out in your relationship with your daughter as she grows up.

On a purely emotional level, you may see someone who will emulate you; someone who will be a special kind of soul mate, who will validate you and pay tribute to who you are. You long for the perfect mother/daughter relationship filling the gaps left in your imperfect relationship with your own mother. If you perceived your relationship with your mother as ideal or very positive, you may long to replicate that relationship.

My friend Helen is at a crossroads with her daughter Rita, now a mother herself. Rita had always been a challenging child, but did grow to become a loving and effective mother. Rita is going through a divorce, and while she makes efforts to become independent and self-sufficient, she occasionally turns to Helen for financial help and physical support. Rita lives in another state, so the physical support is difficult. When Helen has provided financial help she hasn't been happy with how Rita has used the money. That, along with tighter economic times has caused Helen to turn down more recent requests.

Helen recently confided in me that if it weren't for her grandchildren, she would not care to have a relationship with her daughter. When I asked her what she wanted in a relationship with Rita, she said, "I want to have a relationship with my daughter like the one I had with my mother." It turns out Helen longs for someone to be a lot more like herself: independent, assertive, with a single-minded drive to become self-sufficient without help. Helen also admits that she loves the person Rita is on many levels, especially the kind of mother she is to her children. It's not that Helen doesn't want a relationship with Rita; she just doesn't know how to deal with her own frustration and how to respond to the differences between them.

Helen is a good example of someone who is trying to reconcile the two sides of herself: the emotional, more primitive side, and the logical/maternal good mother. She uses a common but ineffective coping mechanism to deal with her disappointment. She distances herself and sees her daughter's actions as a personal affront to her values. In effect, Helen is alienating the very relationship she longs to have, not only with her grandchildren, but also with her daughter. Helen's judgmental behavior is her way to avoid feelings she doesn't understand or know how to cope with.

Each of you has your own story about your relationship with your mother and father. When you become a parent the challenge is to *objectively* examine those relationships and what decisions you've made based on your experience. You then need to evaluate those choices in light of who your child is, and what her unique needs and perspectives are that are similar or different to yours.

WHAT MAKES THE MOTHER/DAUGHTER

RELATIONSHIP SO COMPLEX?

LOOKING AT THE RELATIONSHIP FROM BOTH SIDES:

Imagine you have recently arrived in this world. What might your mother be thinking? If she is like many mothers, she will be awed at the creation of a new human being. She will see you as the realization of her maternal yearnings as well as the opportunity to provide love and nurturing. And she will feel the immense responsibility and sense of great power that comes with the formation of a new life.

An infant is a blank template, a chance for you as a new parent to design and imprint your wishes and ideas to create the ideal childhood. Unconsciously, you may see your child as the opportunity to live out your unfulfilled dreams. The dilemma: If your child does become the realization of your dreams, she may remind you of what you didn't or couldn't do yourself. You can feel a mixture of pride, envy, and resentment. If she doesn't live up to your dreams, you can feel a mixture of disappointment, frustration, and relief. The relief comes from recognizing that how she turned out is okay. How the relationship evolves will be influenced by these dynamics.

WHO ARE YOU AS A MOTHER TO YOUR CHILD?

THERE ARE THREE BASIC AND IMPORTANT INFLUENCES

The first is Love:

The primary and most powerful experience you have when you come into this world is with your mother. Ideally, she somehow knows how to provide for your every need—she magically appears to satisfy your hunger, keep you dry, and soothe your tears. You quickly learn (or assume) that your mother knows what you need, when you need it, and what to do about it. This questionable assumption generates your basic definition of love and stays with you well into adulthood.

When my daughter was sixteen, we were discussing a dilemma she was having, I asked her what she wanted. She informed me: "You're supposed to know what I want and give it to me without me having to ask." We even apply this fantasy of love to our life mates. Many people believe if they have to ask for what they need, their parent/mate doesn't really love them enough or they would somehow know. They further complicate matters by saying, "If I ask for and get what I want, how can I trust it is genuine?"

There is also the kind of mother who can't love, or doesn't know how to love. She may be neglectful or distant and cold, even punishing and abusive. A discussion of these types of mothers and how they affect your notions of love, identity and parenting are described in the section on Parenting Styles.

I believe most mothers truly love their children. This is an important prerequisite for the highly demanding and complex job of parenting, one of the biggest responsibilities you can encounter in life. It is with every good intention you take on the huge role to nurture and shape your child's life.

As a mother, how do you describe the powerful feelings of love you have for your children? What is the particular source and significance of your love for your child? Give this some thought, as it has direct influence on how you parent your child. For example, your love may be the indescribable awareness that you have created another human being, and the responsibility you have taken on to nurture and protect a helpless little infant yet to develop into a person. The power of the bonding experience and the immense obligation of becoming a parent is a byproduct of your biology and the human need for connection.

In some instances a mother, does not develop a bond with her child, perhaps due to her own damaged childhood. She may feel love for her child, and sees an opportunity to heal her own childhood wounds, essentially re-parenting herself. The focus is in large part, on herself and her own needs. In the most extreme situations, particularly for someone who has deep narcissistic wounds, the love for her child is in essence, a manifestation of her own unmet needs for love. It is an attempt to love herself, using her child as a reflection of herself. This is not real love for the child. For this mother, the child as a separate individual does not exist. Her ability to recognize the difference is extremely difficult, if not impossible. However, the child feels the difference and spends much effort trying to find ways to feel loved, usually to no avail.

For many mothers, the love for her child is selfless and consuming, even to the point of substantial sacrifice of her own feelings and needs. The challenge is to find the appropriate balance between sufficient attention and nurturing to your child and to hold on to your own sense of self in the process. For the mother who abandons herself totally, there is a price to pay. You as a mother and a person, have your own nurturing needs that get neglected. When this happens, you deplete yourself of resources and essential energy. You might even develop resentments. Recognizing and creating the necessary balance helps you to be a more effective parent.

The second is Identity:

Early in life, your child sees herself as an extension of you and often tries to imitate your words and actions. It's part of the bonding process. As she grows towards adolescence, her natural developmental process requires her to gradually find her own identity in order to prepare herself for independent adulthood. She may want to emulate her mother in some ways, and also needs to find out how she is different. In addition to the hormonal adjustments, and changes that occur in the child's still developing brain, this is pretty much what teen-age rebellion is about. Your child may feel she has to experiment with extremes to clearly define her boundaries and her sense of self apart from mother. As a mother, you will likely recognize these behaviors with both daughters and sons.

The third is Parenting:

How you decide on what kind of parent you will be is in large part determined by how you evaluate your own experience with your parents. Whether you realize it or not, as a child, you evaluate and store your reactions to the styles your parents practiced. As a daughter, you see your mother as a positive and/or negative role model, and make many life decisions based on what you perceive. You will often select specific traits and behaviors you want to repeat while deciding to avoid or modify others.

If you are a new mother or have plans on becoming a mother, how will you decide what kind of mother you want to be? Some of you will have seen your mother as an ideal role model; some of you will have seen your mother as an unacceptable role model, and some of you will fall somewhere in between these two extremes. For better or worse, most women emulate or reject aspects of what they see in their mothers, and assume what they pass on to their children will be better.

Even if you see your mother as an ideal role model, chances are there are some things, major or minor, you decide you will do differently when you become a mother.

In my own childhood, I had a mother who loved to talk about herself and didn't listen. I decided I would not do that to my children and committed myself to be an attentive and available listener. I thought I had been successful until one day, at age 16, my daughter said to me: "Mom. There's something you do that I really hate—you never talk about yourself."

There is a fourth influence which occurs as your child becomes an adult: Letting Go

How and when you relinquish your job as parent impacts your effectiveness as a parent. and affects your future relationship with your child.

Why might you hold on to your "parenting" role as your child moves into adulthood? Do you do it to fulfill your own needs? Are you engaged in your own struggle to move on? Either way, the message you send your child is, "You aren't capable of functioning as an adult, you still need my help."

When you persist in maintaining your "position" by continuing to give unsolicited advice, opinions and "help," there are consequences. Your child may not learn to take sufficient responsibility for her life. As an emerging adult she may feel pressure to define and preserve her own boundaries. You will always be your child's mother, but at some point you need to relinquish the role of parent.

As a daughter, when you spend time and energy in efforts to please your mother as a way to maintain the childhood bond, you compromise your own development as an adult. If you continue to regularly put your mother first it can interfere with your own effectiveness when you become a parent. As a daughter, letting go involves learning to take responsibility for *your* life. It requires you to find a new way of being with your mother, such as finding ways to relate to each other as two adults. (This issue will be explored further in the section on Letting Go.)

Chapter 5:

THE ROLE OF THE FATHER

Not only are our parenting styles influenced by our upbringing and our early environment, they are also influenced by our mates, and our reactions to how they choose to parent.

In most committed relationships, one person has more power than the other. It is more than a simple dominance/submission issue. My aunt once told me, as I was in the process of searching for a mate: "Make sure he loves you more than you love him." It was her way of telling me to take the power. There are myriad ways power is manifested in a relationship: anger, withholding, passivity, manipulation, guilt, control, pressure, and criticism. In effect, each threatens the partner's security and safety.

Your self-esteem is a major influence on how you deal with the differences and stresses in your relationship. Another significant factor is money. Each mate has his or her own perception of how money affects the power balance. The person who feels less power may compensate for the disparity by becoming more vocal, aggressive, or manipulative (forms of rebellion). He or she may accommodate or compromise often (forms of acquiescence).

As a spouse, you bring your own unique history, life experiences, and philosophy of parenting to the relationship. Even with couples who seem to be very compatible, differences in values and attitudes on child rearing may surface. The disparity can be an opportunity to learn or it can produce tension and disagreement. Serious conflict in the relationship can result. Your differences often come from each of your very deep and personal values. If your mate challenges the way you parent, it can trigger your vulnerability more than most issues. If each of your unique histories is not recognized, acknowledged, and addressed, it could complicate your interactions and spell trouble for the relationship.

The following are some examples of how the marital relationship influences the way you parent:

I. Nancy and Steve are a couple very much in love. They are both smart, loving and kind, devoted parents; they have many talents and strong personalities. Steve has become very successful in his career due to a lot of effort and a lot of smarts. Nancy had a successful career which she gave up when the children came along. She still works part time and is active in many community organizations. Their three children, all entering adolescence, are thriving, along with the typical challenges and upheavals that come with growing up.

Over the years, Steve's demands on his children to get top grades and excel in their extra-curricular activities have influenced the way Nancy parents them. She has largely adopted Steve's parenting style. Nancy is generally outspoken, confident, and willing to stand up for herself. Somewhere along the way, she relinquished some of her own parenting philosophy to accommodate Steve. She may have done it to keep the peace, or because she was unconsciously reacting to Steve's financial power, or both. Whatever the reason, the relationship dynamic has modified her own parenting behaviors.

II. Fran is a sweet, loving, intelligent and accommodating person. Her husband Bill is congenial, loving, smart and full of good intentions. Bill is also a perfectionist and very controlling, to the point of some obsessive and rigid behaviors. He makes many demands on his children and exhibits harsh and sometimes verbally abusive behavior. He is unwilling to recognize or take responsibility for his dysfunctional behavior. Fran, a naturally nurturing and encouraging parent, has been distressed by Bill's insensitivity. In order to compensate, she became overly protective of her children. To her credit, she learned to stand up to Bill, which caused much friction in their relationship. As a result of their parents' conflicting styles which impaired their objectivity, the children were not taught healthy boundaries or adequate coping mechanisms by either parent.

III. Alexa is a bright but somewhat fearful woman, and lacks confidence in her own abilities. She is warm and compassionate by nature, but has become increasingly distant. Her husband Frank, is a dominating presence in the family's life. Not only is he large in size, he speaks with a booming voice and has a stern and demanding manner. He is smart, successful in his business and thinks he knows best in all matters pertaining to work and home life. Alexa feels overwhelmed by Frank, and at a loss to know how to deal with him. Their three children are also very intimidated by their father and look to their mother for support and direction which is not forthcoming.

Alexa's way of coping with her silent, sullen and uncommunicative husband is to run away. She spends a large amount of time pursuing outside activities. She has become very active in a variety of community groups, gets together with friends on a daily basis and even had an affair.

When she is at home she "hides" by reading, watching TV and frequently makes herself unavailable to her children.

Their children feel neglected and have begun acting out. One has become very withdrawn, another has turned to dying her hair purple and pink, getting her body pierced in several places, and being generally uncooperative and angry in an effort to get attention. The third child has taken on the job of being the surrogate parent, telling her siblings what to do, and is very bossy with friends as well. She tries to be Miss Perfect with her parents, pleasing them at every opportunity. The three daughters are all under the age of fourteen. Alexa's friends have encouraged her to leave Frank, which she tried to do twice but ended up going back because she was not confident enough to go it alone.

Chapter 6:

UNCONDITIONAL LOVE

What magic these two words have for us! They are a common dream of all children and the goal of most parents. When you hold your newborn in your arms, the feeling of overwhelming love stirs your heart to vow your unconditional love for this miracle of life. What is unconditional love? What does it mean to you? For many people, it means no matter what my child does, I will love her—without reserve. What if your child became a serial killer, an addict, a prostitute—would you feel the same toward her? What form does your love take then? It's a very tough question. Your idealistic mind might say, "Of course I will still love her, even if I don't approve of her actions." If only it were that uncomplicated.

Unconditional love is defined as affection with no limits or conditions; complete love.[13] Most people interpret unconditional love as a love that will be there, no matter what. We long for the idea of unconditional love as a way to feel safe. It's easy to understand how this notion comes up when you become a parent. You likely want to provide complete security for your child, and your child needs to trust the people who are responsible for her survival.

When we talk of unconditional love, there are two perspectives: one is the point of view of the parent, the other is the perception of the child.

One of the fantasies a mother has is that her child will love her unconditionally. It may even look like that dream has been realized in the early years. The child understands she is dependent on her parent for her very survival. She will therefore do whatever she senses or thinks will please Mom in order to make her world safe. She also sees Mom as a role model and how she learns about the world. It works pretty well until the daughter begins to discover the world outside of her mother, home, and family. As she is exposed to teachers, peers, and other influences she becomes aware of her own emerging place in the community outside her home. She begins to explore the idea of being a separate person from her mother. The process can start as early as pre-school.

When a daughter enters adolescence, she begins a more active process of finding her separate identity. This is a time when hormonal changes and physical development make her look and feel different than the child she's been. Her relationship with peers becomes more important to her than the family ties of childhood.

Often Mom continues to hope for the fulfillment of her fantasy. However, her dreams of receiving unconditional love from her child usually get shattered during this time. No wonder there is such turmoil during this phase. The parent is challenged with coping with her child's development as well as a new phase in her own growth.

Why is unconditional such a universal desire? The answer lies in what you hope and dream will be the effects of this kind of love. You may anticipate that receiving unconditional love will make you feel valued, protected, and secure in your world, as well as giving you the confidence you need to accomplish your goals. You may think it will help you to be courageous in the face of challenges or adversity. You hope it will ensure never being rejected or at least never to be bothered by rejection. You assume it will make you feel unique and special.

From the parent's perspective, giving or receiving unconditional love is a real possibility. Even if this is true for the parent, the child will not necessarily have the same view. What does your child hear the first time you need to say "no"? Does she hear something she has said or done is not okay? Does she hear you placing conditions on your love? When you get impatient, disapprove, or become angry at something she does, your child likely feels she has lost your love, no matter how temporary. Her bubble of unconditional love has burst.

At a very early age, the child starts to look for cues as to what pleases or displeases her parent. She knows pleasing her parent prompts a positive response and displeasing fuels a negative response. She equates these responses with how much she is loved. In the child's view, the parent's love and approval constitutes survival. The fear is: "If my parent doesn't love me, she might abandon me" (physically or emotionally). The young child knows she is not equipped to manage life on her own, so pleasing her parent is the way she ensures her safety in the world. If the parent sees herself as loving her child unconditionally, and the child's perception is different, what are the implications? At the very least, it will produce confusion and tension for both.

The theory of unconditional love implies you are wonderful just as you are. You feel accepted for all you feel, think, and your basic sense of being. No matter what you do, it doesn't jeopardize your worth or value to the other person. You may even assume you are incapable of doing anything wrong. This version of unconditional love requires denial in seeing who the other person really is—human.

There's another side to the story. From your child's perspective: if she does something wrong, (e.g. goes against societal or family norms) and you act as if you didn't notice or simply accept her behavior, your child may think you are not paying attention, caring enough or trusting her enough to confront her actions. She knows she has misbehaved, and when you don't address this it will affect her level of trust towards you.

Ironically, setting healthy and appropriate limits for your child, which can initially appear as an expression of conditional love, has the effect of making your child feel protected and safe. While she may test those limits, she is in actuality checking to see if you love her enough to keep her safe.

UNCONDITIONAL LOVE AND THE DIFFICULT CHILD. A child can be challenging due to distortions of perception, mental deficiency or other systemic issues. How might the lack of unconditional love explain children who are regularly rebellious or uncooperative? For some children, their behavior comes from having given up on being able to please the parent. The child is likely to think or say, "Nothing I do pleases my parent, so why bother." She may think, "My parent never notices me or my efforts to be good." In this instance the child is so desperate for attention, she will do whatever seems to work. Negative attention can make her feel noticed. The rebellion can also be a plea to get the parent to set stronger limits.

On the path to developing her identity, the child needs feedback from others to validate her worth, her existence. Imagine never looking in a mirror, never seeing a photo of yourself, never knowing what you look like. How would you then describe your physical appearance to someone else? You would have to rely on, "the mirror of others' eyes." The child adopts, minimizes, discards or defends behaviors according to the reactions of others. Even when positive behaviors go unnoticed and destructive actions get negative attention, she feels seen, tangible—her existence is confirmed. The negative attention is preferable to feeling a lack of existence, a very frightening prospect.

The process of socialization requires the parent to teach her child coping skills and set boundaries in order to ensure she will function in the world. As you will recognize in some of the Parenting Styles, the parent who attempts to be true to *her* concept of unconditional love can actually do harm to her child. She may neglect to provide the necessary skills to help her child survive and thrive for fear she will upset her child and tarnish the image of unconditional acceptance she wants to portray.

Humanistic psychologist Carl Rogers spoke of an unconditional positive regard (a more realistic interpretation of unconditional love). Rogers stated that the individual needs an environment that provides them with genuineness, authenticity, openness, self-disclosure, acceptance, empathy, and approval.[14]

Abraham Maslow talked about the concept that in order to grow, an individual had to have a positive perspective of him/herself.[15]

If the parent is able to be objective, she is likely to see the teaching of survival skills as a function of her unconditional love. The child at first glance may see those lessons as lack of unconditional love, until she can tangibly experience the benefits. Perhaps you can see why the notion of unconditional love is so complex.

Chapter 7:

THE BONDING EXPERIENCE

The early months and years of a child's life are consumed with the mission of bonding with her mother. The bonding process creates security for the child, and her first experience of trust. Bonding also helps the mother feel motivated to provide the necessary nurturing and stamina to survive the loss of sleep and other deprivations that accompany this stage. The very nature of bonding is attachment. Think of a piece of fabric that is bonded to another piece of fabric. The two pieces are inseparable, and it is difficult to see the edges, where one leaves off and the other begins.

Whether as a parent or child, some of us may recall with fondness that blissful state of feeling as *one.* It is the ultimate sense of not being alone in the world. No wonder so many parents and children have difficulty letting go of that special experience. The infant is literally connected to her mother in the womb, and receives all her nourishment from her mother's body. Once the umbilical cord is cut and the child begins to receive nourishment on her own, it is still often in the form of milk from her mother's body. At some point the child needs to be weaned from the dependence on her mother, and to take nourishment from other sources in the environment. This is true whether we are talking about food or other experiences.

As the child grows and develops, adjustments in the mother/child bond are necessary. A different kind of attachment is required so the child can begin to cultivate her own identity and expand her world. A very significant challenge for the mother and the child is to learn how to remain loving and supportive while allowing the ties of the bond to soften. Knowing when and how to encourage this transition is difficult and delicate. The mother must give up her own investment in the solidity of the bond without appearing to reject her daughter. The mother ideally takes the time and energy to recognize cues of readiness from her daughter and act on them. It can feel like a loss to both mother and daughter. If she pays attention to the needs described in the developmental stage her child is going through, the transition will be easier. Erikson's stages can be a helpful guide in navigating a healthy progression. *(Note: Refer back to the Erikson chart In Chapter 3[8]).*

The issue of boundaries is one of the complexities with many of the Parenting Styles. If the mother is not aware of or committed to loosening the bond, problems occur. The behavior of the parent moves from functional to dysfunctional when she crosses the line between helpful, accepting, or encouraging to demanding, pressuring, controlling, or manipulating.

The parent can lose sight of who she is and who her daughter is as separate and distinct individuals. She may fail to notice and/or respect her daughter as someone who has different needs, different interests, and even a different view of the world. The mother can get caught up in an effort to compensate for her feelings of inadequacy through her daughter. Mother may look to her daughter to emulate her as a means to validate and strengthen her self-worth. Her rationale is, if her daughter follows in her footsteps, it will affirm mother is okay.

Boundaries also get distorted or violated if a mother begins to copy her daughter. A mother may start off by dressing herself and her young daughter in matching outfits and may end up trying to dress like her daughter during teen years and beyond. The imitation can take many other forms as well: picking the same foods off the menu at a restaurant, taking up the same activities such as dancing, sports or other hobbies, and trying to become a friend to her daughter's friends rather than a mother figure.

A mother does this either because she is hoping their similarities will solidify their bond or because she has difficulty defining her own sense of self and looks to her daughter to help identify her own wants, needs, and interests.

The more the mother has learned about herself and has developed a solid sense of her own personality and a comfort level with who she is, the less likely these above scenarios will occur. She will not need to "piggy back" or blur her identity with her daughter. She is able to see the boundaries between herself and her daughter more clearly. She can accept the differences between them as something natural, healthy and desirable. She is ready and willing to accept responsibility for her actions and allows her daughter to take responsibility for her actions as a separate individual. The mother has incorporated the lessons she learned and allows her child to experience the consequences of her own actions. She will neither overprotect nor judge her daughter for her choices, but rather guide and support her daughter in the learning that comes with having her own experiences.

As you read the case examples presented, see if you can identify how and when you set boundaries and what the outcomes might be.

Chapter 8:

CONTROL AND BOUNDARIES

You may notice the issue of control appears in many of the styles described in Chapter 10, the Parenting Styles Inventory. Control is a basic need for all of us to help navigate the unsteady terrain that is our psyche and the unpredictability of the world in which we live. Every parenting style listed is an attempt to have control over our environment in ways we learned or adopted by design or accident. Some styles appear to be anything but controlling.

For example, the Helpless or Dependent Parent attempts to control her environment by getting others to take charge or do things for her, including her children. The Martyr strives to control her environment by pleasing everyone in hopes they will like her and in turn give her what she needs. The Critical Parent or Abusive Parent seeks to take charge by force as a way to get others to do her bidding. The parent may be unaware her actions are an effort to control. In a misguided way, she hopes to feel validated. If she is successful, she may feel satisfied and powerful-- at least temporarily.

Each of the parent's efforts is likely to backfire at some point. Even with your child, you ultimately do not have control over her life. You do have great influence, but it's not the same. You may live with the illusion of control until your child becomes a teen or adult. Then it is payback time. The repercussions are usually expressed through rebellion, withdrawal, estrangement or other forms of acting out.

Worry and anxiety come with the job of parenting and will occur to a greater or lesser degree depending on the Parenting Style you practice. In recognition of the huge responsibility you have taken on, and a desire born out of immense love, you want to do the job as effectively as possible. *Worry is a form of attempting to control your environment; it is a kind of magical thinking.* The state of worry is a clear sign of feeling out of control.

Each person has her own way of dealing with worry. Some ignore it and pretend it doesn't exist. Others seek to make it go away by trying to "fix" or manipulate factors in the environment. And some simply give in to it and live with constant stress. Worry and anxiety are absorbing states of mind and can cause you to lose your objectivity. It gets in the way of your ability to function as effectively as you need to or want to. Unintentionally, you can pass your worry on to those you love who then feel a need to "take care of you," in an effort to soothe your concerns. This can shift the focus away from the person who needs the attention back on to you.

Worry is an activity that is either past or future-based. Whenever you worry, you have left the present moment where you actually have the most control. When you focus on the past for example, you ruminate about something you did or said and what effect it had. When you focus on the future, you make assumptions, usually negative, and imagine what could happen. When you are mentally in the past or the future, you have little control over events. When you stay in the present moment you have the best opportunity to be in charge of your distress. The practice of Mindfulness Meditation[16] has demonstrated substantial benefits for those who learn how to do this.

Worry can also mobilize you into action, *anything* to get rid of that awful feeling of helplessness. In this instance, worry can have a positive effect as long as it doesn't turn into an attempt to control everyone and everything. The worry might motivate you to get more information, to harness resources both internal and external, such as reaching out to friends and professionals. When you take action, you move yourself back into the present.

You can also practice healthy denial to minimize the worry. An example is when you are waiting for the results of medical tests. Diverting your thoughts to other subjects or activities can save you from making a physical or mental wreck of yourself. The key is to know the difference between what you can do to remedy the concern and what you need to let go of. The way to determine this is to ask yourself, "Is there some tangible action I can take to make things better? If you are waiting for news of a possible diagnosis of a serious illness, you will have plenty of time to get upset if the news turns out bad. If you spend your time worrying and your worst fears are confirmed, you will get upset twice: one while you worry, and two, when you get the bad news. If the news turns out to be good, you've spent all that time and negative energy for no reason.

The only real control we have is with ourselves. Developing an internal sense of control is the key to reduce or eliminate the often unsuccessful tendency to manage other people or events.

When you achieve internal control you reduce anxiety, frustration, and put yourself in charge of your world. An internal sense of control gives you the comfort and confidence to be truly accountable for your life.

You will feel equipped to handle almost any situation that arises and recognize you can survive the most difficult challenges. If you did not learn sufficient coping skills growing up, you are more likely to feel out of control and will try to find ways to compensate.

Most of the Parenting Styles described in this book are examples of how we try to make up for feeling out of control. The sooner you learn sufficient coping skills, the better likelihood you have of developing resilience and feeling in charge of your life. It is a compelling reason to help your child build coping skills early. In addition, when you become resilient, you demonstrate how to develop this ability to your child.

Notes:
1. Mindfulness Meditation is the practice of learning to focus on the present moment. Jon Kabat-Zinn[14] said that **mindfulness** is, "paying attention on purpose, in the present moment, and nonjudgmentally, to the unfolding of experience moment to moment."
2. See Appendix for more information and a check list on Developing an Internal Sense of Control

HEALTHY VS. UNHEALTHY BOUNDARIES

One of the challenges of being an effective parent is to know when and how to set appropriate boundaries. This is a fundamental element in guiding your child on her path to maturity. Setting boundaries is important because it helps your child acquire the framework for exploration of her emerging world. It also facilitates an understanding of the consequences she is likely to experience when those boundaries are not respected.

The expression, "The Terrible Twos," refers to the stage of child development when she actively begins to test what is acceptable and unacceptable behavior. (And regularly tests the patience of the parent!) By the age of two, the child usually has developed enough mobility and use of language to experiment with personal control over her physical skills and a sense of emerging independence (Erikson's Stage Two[8]). Toilet training is one example of how the child begins to test behaviors, both with her own body and with her parent.

A popular discussion topic among mothers is how to toilet train their children. Some of the challenges include the child who refuses to go along with her parent who believes "it is time" for her to be toilet trained. The child's lack of cooperation can be frustrating. The parent may not understand the child who develops a fascination with her own feces is seeking a way to learn about her body. Often these are developmental issues, which involve the child's physiological and emotional readiness. The struggle occurs when the *parent thinks the child is ready*, or when she reacts to the pressures of her own environment (e.g. wanting her child to go to pre-school which requires she be toilet trained.) The parent may also respond to her own experiences of growing up, pressures from family members, friends, and even strangers.

Sylvia, a well-educated and devoted mother, went through this struggle with her first child, caving in to the pressures around her and eager to be relieved of the inconvenience of diaper changing chores. She regularly put Darlene on the toilet as she had been advised. These episodes often ended up with mother yelling and daughter crying. In frustration, Sylvia went to her pediatrician who told her, "Don't worry, she will still get accepted into college." This helped Sylvia to relax; Darlene did get toilet trained well in advance of college. After this experience, when her second and third children came along, Sylvia decided her children would let her know when they were ready. And they did, much sooner than she anticipated. It was easy and free of trauma. Instead of engaging in a battle, her younger children had the freedom to learn more about their bodies and feel a pride of accomplishment.

Another common refrain from the two year-old is her discovery of the word "No." She finds a variety of ways to elicit the "no" response. The kind of reply she gets tells her how far she can go, and it provides her with valuable information about her limits. As the parent, you may feel like it's the most often used word in your vocabulary with your two and three year old child. And, it can be exhausting! When the child repeats a behavior she has been told is not acceptable, and then repeats it again and again, she is merely asking if you mean it. When there is enough consistency in your response, the child will relax and internalize the message. She can tell herself: "Now I feel safe, I know where the boundaries are."

When the child enters adolescence this developmental challenge repeats itself. It's a new phase of learning about herself and her independence while she readies herself to separate from her parents as an emerging adult. It is a period of vacillation for the teen: part of her wants to be an adult, yet she's not quite ready to leave the safety of childhood. The same testing occurs, and while she may try to convince you that setting limits means you are a terrible parent, she secretly needs and wants those limits, as long as they are reasonable and appropriate.

During both of these stages, your tolerance and endurance as a parent is put to the test. It requires you to have a clear understanding of appropriate boundaries. You need to be aware of your child's individual emotional, mental, and biological needs. It's equally challenging to remain objective and not allow your own history, outside influences and personal needs to govern your behavior. And, if you don't have it already, you will need to cultivate patience, lots of it. The more fatigued you are, the harder it will be.

The child can be very convincing in her efforts to get her own way. She can cry, get angry, act out physically, or sulk and withdraw. These are tests to see how firm you are, and where you draw the line. When you buy into the child's reactions and give in or give up, she learns she has a weapon to use that works. While she may act and feel triumphant in the moment, she is secretly disappointed that her strategy worked. She is more likely to repeat the behavior, making your job harder. This is where your *consistency* really gets tested. It's also helpful to know the best words to use, and how to communicate those boundaries clearly and with conviction.

For example, saying "I can't let you do/say that," or "Please don't do/say that," is not as effective as saying, "I'm not willing to let you do/say that," or, "I will not allow you to do/say that." The difference is subtle and your tone of voice is important. The first two examples can communicate a lack of certainty, and the second two examples communicate more authority and confidence. Your tone of voice is revealing: if you are feeling anxious, frustrated or unsure, your message will come across differently than when you are feeling calm and assured (or at least able to fake it). Consistency here means your words, body language and actions match, so your child doesn't get a mixed message. When there is a mixed message, the child will tend to believe the non-verbal message—it's not as consciously controlled. Consistency communicates confidence and promotes trust.

Undoubtedly there will be days when despite all good intentions, you as a parent are not up to the task. As long as this is the exception and not your usual reaction, the child will learn what she needs to. As the parent you can also reflect on the incident and revisit it with your child when she --and you-- are in a better frame of mind. It is okay to tell your child you have rethought your previous discussion and realize it was not the best way for you to handle the situation. Your child will learn you are human, reflection is a healthy process, and changing your mind is okay.

Knowing what boundaries to set, how to set them, and when, is a valuable resource to have. Your awareness will strongly influence the success of your efforts and will affect your relationship in a positive way.

Chapter 9:

LETTING GO, HEALING WOUNDS

There are at least two ways to look at Letting Go. One relates to letting go of your position in any given interaction or conflict to achieve resolution. The other refers to letting go of your role as a parent to maintain a healthy relationship with your child as she moves into adulthood.

The first part, holding on to or letting go of your position in any given interaction, has to do with your need to be in control, to have your own way, to be right, or to win. Some parents see preserving their role as a parent as their responsibility. They confuse the need to be in charge or "right" with guiding or teaching. When your child is able to formulate and experiment with her own ideas or positions, as early as age two, the process of letting go is launched. It reaches a critical stage when she becomes a teen-ager. One of the biggest issues during adolescence is the contest of wits and winning engaged in by so many parents and teens. There are no real winners in these battles.

The second phase of letting go is when you encourage your child to develop her own sense of identity. You need to recognize and acknowledge how your child's values and ideas are in concert or contrast with you. She will react to and learn from you depending on how you respond to her emerging ideas that differ from yours. Is there an honest attempt to truly listen to her, to respect her views, and not need to change them—as long as they do not create harm? When you can acknowledge the value in her views as right for her, without having to modify them, it will be a growth experience for both of you and strengthen the relationship.

There are challenges on both sides. Your teenager is going through the developmental stage of separation and individuation, needing to find out who she is as a separate individual. She will experiment with what it feels like to have thoughts, feelings and ideas different from you. At times she will take this to the extreme, and go as far as possible in a direction opposite to your ideas, values and beliefs. She feels the need to go to extremes to more clearly define her own principles and boundaries.

Examples of this include the teen who colors her hair purple, pierces a variety of body parts, smokes, drinks, engages in risky behaviors, or simply acts out at school or with friends. The motto seems to be, "If my parents won't like this, it's a good reason to do it."

During this time, you experience your own process of separation from your child. Your daughter is making an effort to become less dependent on you. Experiments like those described above are not only unfamiliar, they seem like a rejection of all the values you have tried to instill in your child. It can also feel like a rejection of who you are as a parent and a person.

Pick your Battles: What is not appropriate for you as the parent is to allow all expressions of verbal and acting out behavior. The real test for you is to figure out which behaviors you can tolerate or accept as a normal part of this phase (whether the child is two, thirteen, or seventeen). Can you avoid a contest of wits and wills with your child? As the parent you also need to clarify which behaviors are too risky, ones likely to have serious physical or emotional consequences for your child. You need to set clear limits and avoid overly long or zealous confrontations. You may need the perspective of other adults you respect as being objective, or even a professional. *This does not mean seeking out friends who will agree with you.*

Are you willing and able to let go of dearly held positions? It requires an open mind, a perspective based on understanding the consequences of your actions, and an ego that isn't dependent on always being "right." You need to be objective, to see the issue from the other person's viewpoint, to consider the effect on the relationship, and to know what is at risk.

"Pride goeth before a fall"[17] refers to your need to protect your ego as you see it. The ego can become all-important, often to the point where one person is willing to walk away from a relationship over what may likely be a resolvable issue. When your pride is involved, it can feel like you are fighting for survival of your mind, body and soul. Your awareness of the other person's feelings and needs all but disappears. This position often has consequences you will regret. If you are willing to take a chance and experiment, you may find that subduing your pride doesn't destroy you and can grow or save the relationship.

To put your pride in perspective, choose a situation where the issue is minor, where letting go of your position is manageable for you, even if not pleasant or easy. See what happens when you acknowledge the other person's point of view and agree to drop your well-prepared defense. You might be surprised! If this works well for you, keep practicing until you can move on to more important issues, one step at a time. You just may find the benefits outweigh the discomforts.

The second phase, letting go of the parenting relationship, requires you to recognize and digest the reality you will always be a mother, and at some point you will need to relinquish your role as a parent for the well-being of both your child and you. It is easier said than done.

By the time your child reaches adulthood, being a parent has become a central aspect of your identity. You may have a career, a spouse, close friendships, an avocation, or be involved in the community. Each of these parts of your life contributes to your identity. Your responsibility as a parent is likely one of the most absorbing and time-consuming of all your activities. In addition, it involves someone you love deeply. You likely see yourself as the guardian of her welfare. Letting go of the parenting role can cast you adrift in the waters of uncertainty. Who will you be to your child, and who will she be to you, once you discontinue parenting?

Letting go involves loss—the loss of an important aspect of your identity, of the belief you have control over your child, of the ending of a stage of life, and the historical structure and content of your relationship with your child. It may also raise questions about your marital relationship. When the children leave home, you may have a new challenge: how to reconstitute your relationship with your spouse on the basis of being something other than your children's parents.

Some of the issues and examples addressed in the first part of this section are a requirement for letting go of the parent role. One key is to learn how to discriminate between age-appropriate behaviors for the child and know when to set limits and when to let go. You may have difficulty allowing your child to become her own person—it can feel like you are losing your connection with her and becoming estranged. I've seen many parents who take great pride in their child becoming "just like them" and believe this helps maintain the closeness they've always had. The child who goes along with this may be postponing her development as a separate individual. She might harbor frustration or resentment, even if unconscious. As a result, at some point, usually as an adult, she may withdraw or rebel. This can occur at any stage of adulthood. It is not unusual for it to happen when your daughter becomes a parent.

When you accept and encourage your child/now adult to become her own person you affirm your trust and love for her. When you are willing to let go of the parent/child relationship you had you show her you have confidence in her. This can create a foundation for a new and enriched connection which will be much healthier, valuable and enduring than trying to hold on to the familiar and seemingly safer but unrealistic old relationship.

In the process of letting go, you need to recognize who you are as an individual, what your assets, abilities and dreams are as a unique human being, apart from being a parent. In this regard, your process is a parallel one to your child's. When you can rediscover yourself, your life will be richer and more fulfilling. Your need to *parent* will diminish and your life can become a new journey of discovery. It will allow you to have a more rewarding relationship with your child. You will be able to connect as two adults, even as you maintain the bonds of mother and daughter.

TO LET GO TAKES LOVE

To "let go" does not mean to stop caring; it means I can't do it for someone else.

To "let go" is not to cut myself off; it is the realization that I can't control another.

To "let go" is not to enable, but to allow learning from natural consequences.

To "let go" is to admit powerlessness, which means the outcome is not in my hands.

To "let go" is not to try to change or blame another; it is to make the most of myself.

To "let go" is not to care for, but to care about.

To "let go" is not to "fix", but to be supportive.

To "let go" is not to judge, but to allow another to be a human being.

To "let go" is not to be in the middle arranging all the outcomes, but to allow others to affect their own destinies.

To "let go" is not to be protective; it is to permit another to face reality.

To "let go" is not to deny, but to accept.

To "let go" is not to nag, scold, or argue, but instead to search out my own shortcomings and to correct them.

To "let go" is not to adjust everything to my desires, but to take each day as it comes, and to cherish myself in it.

To "let go" is not to criticize and regulate anybody, but to try to become what I dream I can be.

To "let go" is not to regret the past, but to grow and to live for the future.

To "let go" is to fear less and to love more.

--reprinted with permission from Robert Paul Gilles, Jr. ©1997[18]

HEALING WOUNDS—REPAIRING DAMAGE

Perhaps you are reading this book because your relationship with your child has been an unhappy one for a long time. Hopefully you are at least still speaking to each other, even if it is limited and/or strained. Understanding your Parenting Style can be an important first step in learning what needs to be done to begin the process of repair. The next steps are critical if you are to find a way back to having a more positive relationship with your child.

One of the important lessons I learned as a therapist occurred while listening to women describe their relationships with their mothers. Some relationships appeared to be very damaging, others seemed fairly minor. It was not the severity of the damage that determined the outcome. What changed things between the parent and child was whether or not the mother made an effort to be different, to take responsibility and acknowledge her part in what went wrong. This was a strong message to the daughter that her mother really cared about her and the relationship.

Taking Responsibility – Acknowledge what your part is in creating the relationship as it now exists. Do not avoid responsibility by using "yes, but" explanations. Some examples of this type of reasoning are: "I was very critical of my daughter, but she was always acting out, I didn't know what to do." "She was so lazy and unmotivated, I had to be hard on her," or, "There were so many other things going on in my life, I didn't have the time or energy to do what I needed to." No matter what your reasons, when you take your share of responsibility, it makes it safer for your child to own up to her part as well. This demonstrates goodwill and becomes a bridge to rebuild your relationship.

Another benefit of taking responsibility: you serve as a role model as well as providing an opportunity for honest dialogue. I have seen many standoffs, where each person is waiting for the other to be the first one to acknowledge their part in creating or contributing to the problem. Like opening a door, the person who goes first paves the way and provides safety.

Listening—In addition to taking responsibility, the single most important skill to learn and practice is Active Listening[12] (see Appendix). I have seen these two practices heal more relationships than anything else. Actively listening to your child builds rapport. It sends a strong message that you are truly interested in her perspective, her feelings, her needs and wishes. It also creates "emotional clearance," providing a mental space for your child to be more open to hearing what you want to say. Develop the habit of *listening first* until your child has had the opportunity to fully express what she needs to and feels satisfied she has been sincerely heard. This creates the emotional space to listen without her own agenda interfering.

The writing exercise on Healing Our Relationship in the Appendix section at the end of the book is a tool you can use to help you move through the process in the most productive way possible. When a relationship is strained or worse, communicating by writing letters is a safer way to approach the issues that divide you. By this I mean a handwritten letter. Letters will also help you and your child reflect on what has been expressed without feeling the pressure of being observed, noticing non-verbal judgments or seeing the other person ready to pounce on whatever is said.

Note: E-mails do not convey the thoughtful deliberation that needs to go into these communications, and should not be used when the issue has emotional content. In addition, it is easy to hit "send" too quickly, and then regret it. A handwritten letter sends a message that more thought has gone into the writing, and the subject being addressed is very important. And you have the opportunity to read, re-read, and/or change what you want to express.

Chapter 10:

WHY BECOME A PARENT?

Considerations for Parenting

There are many reasons people decide to have children when they do. For many, it's a romantic notion. This sweet, innocent, and helpless creature will be a vessel for the outpouring of all the love they have to give. For others, it is a means of solidifying the relationship with their spouse, or as an expression of their marital love and commitment. Some people perceive a child as someone who offers a sense of destiny, provides continuity for the family line, or creates a sense of immortality.

And as discussed in the previous section, it is the opportunity for a relationship with someone we believe will love us unconditionally, who will fill all our unmet needs for love, attention, and respect. It's also appealing to have someone who will look to us for guidance, wisdom, and direction. Perhaps we seek someone who will never abandon us, or who will be there to take care of us in our declining years. It might be that we long for someone who can live out all our unfulfilled desires and dreams. Every parent likely has at least some of these quite normal and human thoughts. The question is, to what degree do these ideas influence your decision?

According to Erikson,[19] in order to be an effective parent, one needs to have progressed through and accomplished all the developmental challenges that lead to Stage 7, Generativity vs. Self-absorption. This stage includes having a mate and becoming capable of true intimacy as opposed to isolation. His theory asserts that by going through all the prior stages successfully, you will be ready and able to temporarily abandon your own needs, putting them aside for the sake and well-being of a child. These achievements provide the optimal condition for being a successful parent.

Understanding your underlying motives will help you clarify your intentions. It will make it possible to improve your parenting skills in the areas you recognize as lacking.

It is therefore important to examine your true reasons for your decision to become a parent. You will need to be honest and objective. For a helpful way to assess your motivations, complete the scale that follows, rating yourself on each dimension. You might also want to get some feedback from someone who knows you well, who you trust and who can be objective and honest. You can also ask them to rate you on the following scale.

When one mate wants a child and the other doesn't

This is a subject you need to discuss before you make a commitment to share your life with a partner. The issue will not go away with your statements of unending love for each other. If your desire to have a child is strong, tension can build up over time and end up tearing apart the very fabric of your relationship. Even if the subject is never brought up, it will come out in indirect ways. For example, it may become a test of how much love your mate has for you, or you have for your partner. One partner may make excessive demands on the other to make up for feeling deprived of fulfillment of a basic desire.

One couple I met with had neglected to discuss this before they were married. About three years into their marriage, the husband started talking about having a child. The wife did not want to have children. Their relationship was on solid ground, and they were both very intelligent and open-minded. They recognized the dangers of not resolving this issue. After much dialogue, the wife came to a conclusion. It boiled down to whether she wanted to live with guilt (getting her way) or resentment (living with her husband getting his way). She chose to live with resentment, and they had a child. As it turned out, she was surprised by the great love she felt for her child, and the resentment never came up. It was a creative way to resolve a thorny issue. Fortunately for them, the downside of her decision never happened. Not all couples would be so lucky. It can be a productive way to resolve a complex challenge. To be successful it requires maturity, honesty and sufficient introspection on the part of both partners.

PARENT APTITUDE SCALE

Circle the number that best describes your reasons for becoming a parent: 1= little motivation, 10= very strong motivation:

1. A place to give my love

1 2 3 4 5 6 7 8 9 10

2. To solidify my relationship with my mate

1 2 3 4 5 6 7 8 9 10

3. An expression of love for my mate

1 2 3 4 5 6 7 8 9 10

4. To perpetuate the family line

1 2 3 4 5 6 7 8 9 10

5. A sense of immortality

1 2 3 4 5 6 7 8 9 10

6. To be loved unconditionally

1 2 3 4 5 6 7 8 9 10

7. To be looked up to for guidance and wisdom

1 2 3 4 5 6 7 8 9 10

8. To be able to mold and shape a human being

1 2 3 4 5 6 7 8 9 10

9. Someone who will never abandon me

1 2 3 4 5 6 7 8 9 10

10. To be taken care of in my old age

1 2 3 4 5 6 7 8 9 10

11. Someone who can fulfill my unmet dreams

1 2 3 4 5 6 7 8 9 10

12. To devote myself selflessly to another

1 2 3 4 5 6 7 8 9 10

Other: _____

1 2 3 4 5 6 7 8 9 10

Now look at your responses. What do they tell you about your incentives to become a parent?

If you rated yourself high on numbers 6-11, you may want to re-examine your motivations. If you rated yourself high on numbers 1, 3, 4, and 12, you are more likely to become a successful parent. Number 2, "To solidify a relationship" has its positives and negatives because having a child can result in either enhancing or further stressing the relationship. A child can bring two people closer as an expression of their love for each other (No. 3) or it can drive a wedge between them, creating further stress in a relationship that may already have tension or discord.

It will be helpful for your mate to complete this scale also, to determine his parenting aptitude. If one of you is ready and the other isn't, it can create additional strain and problems in the relationship. If there are issues between the two of you, consider getting some counseling before you commit to becoming parents.

Chapter 11:

INTRODUCTION TO PARENTING STYLES ASSESSMENT

Complete objectivity in deciding how to become the kind of parent we want to be is a huge challenge. In the section on Parenting Styles, you have an opportunity to learn more about your choices and whether they arise from imitation, intimidation, rebellion, rejection, objectivity, or a combination of two or more. The Parenting Styles inventory describes different parenting styles and addresses the implications of each. Armed with this information, you will be better able to evaluate what you are doing, look at your actions more objectively, and decide whether you want to maintain or modify some of your thinking, approaches or behaviors.

It is important to view the Parenting Styles in the context of intensity, frequency, and duration. We all make mistakes as parents, and can find ourselves fitting into several of the categories at times. Parenting Styles refers to patterns of behavior that are your typical ways of interacting with your child, especially when you are under stress. Occasional lapses into any of these behaviors are not necessarily going to have a lasting effect on your child, especially if you pay attention to what you are doing. The exception is when even your occasional actions are severe and physically or mentally harmful. You can reduce the negative impact if you take responsibility and acknowledge your actions and their effect on your child. This needs to be followed up with a real (not temporary) change in your actions and/or attitudes. Engage in a dialogue with your child to explore ways you can make things better. Having the dialogue gives you the opportunity to show your child you are human and make mistakes. You set a good example for how to handle those mistakes. It can also give you an opportunity to reaffirm your love and parental commitment to your child. And, it can create an opening to learn more about you and your child, helping you to discover new ways to improve your parenting.

The Parenting Styles you adopt are in large part based on acceptance, modification, or rejection of your own parent's styles. The influence of society as well as information you receive from books, friends, and other significant people in your life also play a role. You may make a conscious effort to repeat or change your own experience growing up. Even when you seek to create a different experience for your child, you may end up repeating many of the practices you sought to avoid without recognizing you are doing so. You may not realize how much you have internalized some of the interactions you lived with during your formative and impressionable years. You also make decisions based on what you as a child needed and didn't get. You may assume your child needs or wants the same things. You may act more in response to your old unmet needs than to your child's unique personality. It takes courage and an open mind to focus on who your child is as a distinct individual and not assume she has the same needs you did.

There will likely be times when the appropriateness or value of your parenting style is called into question either by you or someone else, and you recognize the need to do something different. A single action or even a short period of new behaviors will not be sufficient to minimize or eliminate the habits you are trying to remedy. Habits are powerful and usually firmly entrenched in your mental and psychological system. It takes on average, eight to twelve weeks of regular and consistent reinforcement of new behaviors to effectively replace those you want to remove[20]. For some it may take even longer, depending on the degree of your motivation and the extent you are entrenched in your habitual behavior. It may even require professional help to understand the difficulty you have in replacing new behaviors for the old.

Your parenting style is also influenced by your own internal conflict between wanting your child to have her own identity, to "be her own person" and the great compliment you feel as a parent when your child chooses to follow in your footsteps. It's a boost to your ego to have your child emulate you-- a validation of your own worth. Her imitation also helps you feel closer and more connected to her. This duality can create an internal struggle regarding your parenting. The temptation is strong, and it's hard to resist giving in to your own gratification and consequent loss of objectivity. Are you able to focus on what you value most in your parenting, and your responsibility to your child? Find ways to remind yourself whenever you are seduced by ego gratification. Ask yourself: "What is most important to me: my ego, my child's well-being and/or the quality of my connection with my child?" These are some of the critical issues in Erikson's stage of development called Generativity vs. Stagnation (also referred to as Self-Absorption[7, 8]). There is no pursuit or calling more likely to bring your values into focus than being a parent.

The descriptions of the parenting styles include possible consequences of how a given style might influence the child's subsequent attitudes and behavior. Remember, each individual is unique, and the effect of a given style is not universal; the descriptions pertain to common reactions. Children can be resilient, defiant, self-sufficient or compliant by temperament and this will influence how they respond to different parenting styles. Some professionals will assert that the qualities of resilience, defiance, self-sufficiency or compliance are inborn; others will maintain they are learned. In either case, children do exhibit these traits early in life and it will affect their reaction to a given style.

Another influence in a child's response is her experiences with other significant people in her life. The other parent, grandparents, aunts, uncles, older siblings, close family friends, teachers or spiritual leaders all have an effect. These other relationships can either intensify or modify the child's reactions.

Each of the Parenting Styles described assume you have great love for your child. As a parent you are the product of your own unique experience. As previously mentioned, how you were parented as a child has a strong influence on the style you choose. Your choice is at least partly based on repeating or imitating the style you were exposed to—or electing to parent in a style very different to what you experienced. This is not always a conscious decision.

Why are there so many more seemingly dysfunctional parenting styles than functional ones? Because we are complex beings and without intending to, we make things more complicated than they need to be. Also, since life is full of stress, we will more likely revert to one of these styles when our stress levels are high or ongoing.

A valuable resource for mastering stress and developing a better understanding of yourself to find more effective ways to communicate with your child—and others—is Emotional Intelligence[21]. EQ or Emotional Intelligence is the process of identifying your emotions and learning how to manage them effectively within yourself and in your interactions with others. Without an understanding of what are feeling, and how to manage those feelings, you are likely to act them out in indirect and/or unproductive ways.

A simple way to remind yourself of your mind set is to employ a *high road/low road* metaphor. When you are feeling good about yourself and able to be centered and objective, you will take the *high road,* the one that will produce the optimal benefit to you and your child. When you are under stress, feeling emotionally shaky (e.g. depressed, frustrated, angry, helpless) you will take the *low road,* the one most likely to prevent you from successfully resolving the problem and may even create new ones. As you are about to address a sensitive issue, before you jump in, ask yourself, "Do I want to take the high road or the low road?" This might be enough to get you on track.

Our complexity comes from myriad influences leading up to the day we become parents and beyond. Our choices as to how we parent come in part from the experiences we have had. They also are the result of the way we react to those experiences and the meaning we assign to them. It is why a child from an abusive or neglectful upbringing can turn out to be a highly functioning and stable adult, while a child from a seeming loving family can turn out to have multiple issues that cause her to struggle with life.

There are also more subtle ways you as a parent affect your child. You can be outwardly loving and supportive, but may harbor resentment or conflicts you attempt to hide or suppress. For example, conflicts can stem from feeling more comfortable raising a son than a daughter because you relate easier to males. You might have been neglected as a child and while you deeply want to heal your past and treat your child differently, you find yourself treating your child the same way you were treated. You might become overprotective, controlling or indulgent. You may also find yourself practicing any one of the dysfunctional Parenting Styles in a misguided attempt to compensate for the negligence you experienced.

It is not the style itself that is functional or dysfunctional. Much depends on the degree and frequency with which the style is used. You will likely relate to several styles—determined by the above factors— how often, to what extent, and under what circumstances the style is applied. A given style becomes dysfunctional when it becomes a regular way you interact with your child, and/or when you notice problem behaviors building up in your child. (A child becoming silent and withdrawn can be one of those warning signs). While the problem behaviors might not come directly from the Parenting Style, it is important to evaluate the possibility of your actions as the source or a contributing factor. In any event, problem behaviors are a red flag that something is happening with your child and needs thoughtful attention.

All too often, parents see the child's behavior as a discipline issue and don't look at how they might be contributing to the problem. A thoughtful, introspective evaluation will help clarify what type of action is called for. Sometimes prompt discipline is required. Even in those instances when things calm down, both you and your child will benefit from sitting down and reviewing the incident. Truly listening to your child with an open heart is essential to learning from the experience*. It requires you to ask open-ended questions (avoid those that can be answered with "yes" or "no"). Also avoid questions beginning with, "Why," (because this can put the child on the defensive). You will encourage a better response when you start with "I'd really like to understand what you were thinking or feeling." You can also say, "It would be helpful to know what you need." Allow your child to speak freely without interruption or jumping in with comments or advice. Take responsibility for your part in the outcome. You and your child have the best opportunity to learn from the experience when you take advantage of this opportunity.

Notes:
1. Consistent practice of any new behaviors is a challenge. On average, it takes more than two months before a new behavior becomes automatic – sixty-six days to be exact. And how long it takes a new habit to form can vary widely depending on the behavior, the person, and the circumstances (Lally, van Jaarsveld, Potts and Wardle[20])
2. See Appendix on Effective Communication[12]

VIRGINIA SATIR

Virginia Satir (1916-1988)[22], was one of the pioneers and sages of family therapy. She developed a model for behaviors to represent ways people use to get around threats to their self-esteem and sense of well-being. In her book on communication and relationships: Peoplemaking, she introduces the theory of Patterns of Communication. Her model applies to interactions with other people, and is included in aspects of the parenting styles you will be reading about. Her theory includes the following four basic dysfunctional styles: Placater, Blamer, Computer, and Distracter. Her fifth style which is the functional style, is the Leveler.

For example, you will find elements of the Placater in the Overprotective Parent, the Helpless or Dependent Parent, the Martyr, and the Smothering Parent Styles. Aspects of the Blamer may be occur in the Critical Parent, the Overachieving Parent, the Defensive, Competitive and Abusive Parenting Styles. The Computer can be seen in the Unemotional and Controlling Parent Styles. Facets of of the Distracter will be manifested in the Indirect, Controlling, and Laissez-Faire Parent Styles. The Leveler will be evident in the Nurturing, Encouraging and Cooperative/Collaborative Parent Styles.

Take some time to reflect on how your parents raised you. What are the qualities and actions they expressed that you consciously decided to emulate? What are the qualities you consciously decided not to emulate or to do the opposite? Have you been able to follow through with your intentions? Are there some qualities you have repeated, in spite of all your promises to yourself you would not? Refer back to the exercise Exploring and Understanding our History.

Note: Virginia Satir (1916 –1988) was an American author and social worker known especially for her approach to family therapy and her work with family reconstruction. She is widely regarded as the "Mother of Family Therapy"[1][2] Her most well-known books are *Conjoint Family Therapy*, 1964, *Peoplemaking*, 1972, and *The New Peoplemaking*, 1988.

NOTES ON HOW TO VIEW PARENTING STYLES

The twenty Parenting Styles you will be exploring are mainly based on emotional responses with the exception of three, which are mainly based on objective processes. The descriptions show extreme examples of each style in order to highlight the issues involved. Most people will not fit these strong portrayals. You may find a combination of styles or aspects of styles that apply to your own upbringing. See if you can figure out what the predominant style was, and which ones were present but less influential. Notice that what you experienced may be a modification of the description. Strong feelings from the past might come up for you as you explore these styles. If this happens, it's an indication your reactions are continuing to influence your relationships with others, whether they are your children (even if they are now adults), mates, or even friends and co-workers.

As parents and as humans, we have myriad reactions to events and to our environment. By identifying where you are on the scale of each style, you can then plot a grid (a form for this is at the end of the Parenting Styles section) which will reveal your predominant tendencies. The biggest challenge will be honesty. I assume if you are reading this, you want to be the best parent you can be. Your strong desire can make it difficult to recognize actions on your part that are different from what you wish for. Looking inward with authenticity is a critical component if you are to achieve your goal. You need to be willing to recognize where you fall short. If you take responsibility for your shortcomings, you enable yourself to do something about them. When you avoid responsibility and awareness, you render yourself helpless to make the positive changes necessary for your desired results. It is also important *not to demand or expect* you will ever be the perfect parent, or perhaps even as good as you long to be. The harm to your child comes from consistently parenting in dysfunctional ways. The occasional lapse is human and will be an example to your child that making mistakes is a natural and acceptable part of being human. It is also one of the best opportunities you have for learning. The motto I live by is: *Nothing is ever a mistake if you learn from it.*

As my children grew into young adults, I often asked them for feedback on my parenting, even when I knew I wouldn't like what they said. I believe I could not become a better parent unless I understood their perspective. I wanted to learn what was helpful and what was not. It didn't mean I gave them all the power or even agreed with what they said. It definitely didn't mean I was turning over the responsibility of my parenting to them. It simply meant I wanted to see the world from their point of view which often was quite different from mine.

What really mattered to them was my willingness to enter into their world view and develop a sense of how they experienced events. The "truth" as I saw it was irrelevant. Our perceptions are our reality, so for each of us there will be a different "truth" when we recall or respond to actions or events. Our children develop their coping mechanisms, attitudes and behaviors according to their experience and instincts, not *our* version of reality. If you really want to understand and connect with them, it is necessary to suspend your attachment to your own viewpoint, at least long enough to view things through their eyes and listen to what they hear.

Often the healing of old hurts occurs when your child takes in the message you truly "know" what they experienced, not simply on an intellectual level, but on an empathic feeling level. One of the greatest compliments a parent can receive is her child saying, "You really understand. You 'get' me!"

Chapter 12:

THE PARENTING STYLES INVENTORY

THE CRITICAL PARENT

Description:

A Critical Parent is one who regularly judges, discounts, puts down, and blames her child (and others) for everything. She continually focuses on the negative. In the parent's mind, she does this out of love. Her goal is to teach her child what is "right" by telling her what she is doing wrong. She believes that's the best way for her child to learn. She may even feel guilty if she fails to point out her child's errors in thinking, judgment, or action, perceiving it as neglecting her parental obligations.

One possible source of this style is what the parent learned in her own family of origin and simply repeats what she experienced. Another possibility is the parent came from a family who was very lax in teaching her as a child to the point of benign neglect. The child grew up believing her parents didn't care since they showed little or no interest in helping her acquire fundamental life skills. As a parent, she lacked the information she needed to help her child develop appropriate life tools. So she decided to do the opposite. Moreover, since she was never exposed to positive reinforcement she didn't pass that on either

In its extreme form, a child raised in a critical environment grows to believe she can't do anything right. Whatever she does never seems good enough. The Critical Parent may single one child out for this treatment or she may be this way with everyone. Even if the child is not the focus of her parent's criticism, she can still be affected if she observes it on a daily basis in her parent's treatment of siblings or others. She might have thoughts like: "Wow, I'm lucky she's not coming after me." "I wonder when it will be my turn." She may at turns feel fortunate, guilty for being spared or sad for her sibling who is the object of her parent's criticism. In addition, her sibling may resent or envy her. Whether or not the child is the object of the criticism, she might try extra hard to please mother, hoping to avoid becoming the target. Even if only one person is being singled out, it influences the entire family's dynamic.

Effects on Child:

The effects of criticism on a child are varied. The most obvious is damage to the child's self-esteem. She begins to see herself as being inadequate. She can become fearful of taking action, speaking up or making decisions. She may develop shyness or a need to please others. She tries to change what she perceives as others' opinions of her. She might become depressed, sullen or rebellious—typical of a child who has given up and believes she can never please anyone, so why try.

The child of a critical parent can also become critical of others, especially younger siblings or friends. She may seek out people she thinks she can influence. They become an outlet for her frustration and a way to vent her anger on those she considers safe. Because she is too young and inexperienced to determine how justifiable the criticism is that she receives from her parent, she assumes the "charges" are valid. This is particularly true for the very young child who needs to see her parents as all-knowing in order to keep her world safe. If the criticism becomes unbearable at some point, she will try to lessen the impact on herself by becoming judgmental of others. It is a misguided attempt to build herself up at the expense of others.

Examples:

I. On the mild end of the scale, the parent will deliver criticism and try to balance it with praise. Benita's mother believed criticism was the best way to teach her child—if she didn't call attention to what Benita was doing wrong, how would she ever learn not to do those things? She would point out Benita's mistakes, errors in thinking or judgment, and also at times, make an effort to recognize and comment on Benita's accomplishments. Benita did not suffer the more extreme negative consequences, and when the criticism and compliments were in balance, she was pretty okay with it all. Because of this, Benita was able to take the criticism as a learning experience and not an evaluation of her self-worth.

II. Polly had a mother who was a perfectionist. Her mother, with all good intentions, tried to create the "perfect" child in Polly. Even though Polly was very bright, her mother continually tried to improve on whatever Polly did. Praise always came with a "but": "That's very good, but have you thought of doing this to make it better?" If she was asked to pick up her toys, and complied as a two-year old would, she was told "You're not doing it fast enough." As a result, Polly didn't get to enjoy the fruits of her efforts and was left feeling she could never get it right. Polly became confused about what was expected of her. She never knew when she would get reprimanded for something she thought she was doing satisfactorily or even very well. She began to anticipate what might possibly be wrong with almost everything she did. She became hyper-vigilant, nervous, and fearful. She began to apologize for simple mistakes, even events she didn't cause. All the reassurance she received from her father and other extended family members didn't help. In her young mind, anticipation was the best way she could figure out how to protect herself from the inevitable criticism.

III. Hillary's mother Allison, suffered from feelings of inadequacy as a parent. She was continually fearful of doing or saying the wrong thing. So she covered it up with criticism, pretending she always knew what was right. Allison's anxiety caused her to be hyper-critical, providing her with many opportunities to demonstrate her "knowledge." If Hillary had been willing to become totally submissive to her mother, things would have gone more smoothly. Hillary however, like most children, was eager to discover who she was. She tested limits to learn where the boundaries were, what was okay, and what wasn't. Hillary wanted to see if her mother meant what she said, a normal and natural part of child development. Each time Hillary would test her limits, she was met with a barrage of criticism and punishment. Allison saw her daughter's actions as questioning her parental abilities, which struck at the core of her insecurities. This only increased the criticism. Hillary eventually learned to back off and became more compliant. As a result her personality development suffered. She became quiet and shy. She avoided experimenting with new behaviors. It was easier to follow the "rules" and avoid the verbal onslaught.

Helpful Hints:

Criticism in some form is pretty inevitable, even with the best intentions to reinforce positive behavior. In these cases, it is a knee-jerk reaction often based on emotion rather than logic.

When you are tired, preoccupied or otherwise not at the top of your game, you will not have the patience and creativity to be able to think through the most effective way to handle the situation.

A helpful remedy is to recognize the criticism, even if it is a day or a week later, and engage in a dialogue with your child. Ask her what feelings she experienced in response to your unsympathetic comment. For example, "I realize I said some things that weren't very kind or helpful. Can you tell me how it felt to you?" It's an opportunity for you to learn more about your child and how she reacts to your parenting style. You can *then* apologize for the *way you handled the situation*, thus showing your child that it's human to make mistakes. You can also ask your child what helps her learn the best. This type of conversation communicates caring in a concrete way, more effective than simply saying, "I'm sorry," "I love you," or "I care about you."

A word of caution: It is important to draw out your child's feelings *before* you apologize. A quick "I'm sorry" can be seen by the child as an attempt to cut off the expression of her feelings. The dialogue needs to take place when you are in a centered place, coming from empathy, not guilt. Your tone of voice and body language will reflect how you are feeling inside, and your child will pick up on this. You need to be feeling authentic, truly okay with yourself, comfortable and confident in your role as parent.

Directions for the exercise below (this scale follows each parenting style): Circle the number that best describes the extent of your participation in this style.

1 equals minor involvement, 10 equals a high degree of involvement. Do the same for your mother, father, and spouse.

Critical Parenting Scale

Mother	1	2	3	4	5	6	7	8	9	10
Father	1	2	3	4	5	6	7	8	9	10
Spouse	1	2	3	4	5	6	7	8	9	10
Me	1	2	3	4	5	6	7	8	9	10

THE OVERPROTECTIVE/SMOTHERING PARENT

Note: These two styles have many similarities, and a few differences which are described here. For this reason, there are two rating scales to allow you to address each aspect separately.

Description:

The Overprotective and/or Smothering Parent will control, over-anticipate (especially negative outcomes), over-empathize, martyr herself, or be excessively affectionate. She will not allow her child to make mistakes, fall down, feel bad, or handle her own conflicts/disputes with others. This style has often been referred to as the Helicopter Parent.

One of the most difficult distinctions for many parents to make is the line between love and overprotection. For these parents, next to the word "good parent" in the dictionary is the description of "overprotective." Your great love for your child, as well as your sense of biological, social, and emotional responsibility, is to protect your offspring from harm or danger. It becomes unclear at times what is real harm or danger and what is perceived harm or danger. You long to save your child from pain, both physical and emotional. You are strongly tempted to jump in when you anticipate or assume there is physical and/or emotional injury. From your child's very early years, you may discourage her natural curiosity to explore if you anticipate she could get into trouble.

Your child might fall, hurt her head, or scrape her knees or elbows. She might break a favorite vase, rip pages out of your books, draw on the wall or destroy the expensive toy you just bought her. In the name of loving guidance you save her from all of this by watching over her with your words of caution or discouragement. As she grows a little older, you save her from the embarrassment of poor grades by helping her with her homework, make many decisions for her, and convince her to avoid taking risks.

Of course your job is to socialize her; to teach her responsibility, discipline, and to provide structure. Where do you draw the line? How much do you do for her that she is capable of doing for herself? To what extent do your own fears, your own needs, and your own childhood experiences of being under- or over-protected influence how you are with her? How willing are you to let her grow up and away from you? How much do you need to be in control of her life as compensation for being out of control of your own? To what extent do you protect her because you have difficulty tolerating physical and/or emotional discomfort in yourself--or anyone else? To what extent do you believe pain is something that should be avoided whenever possible? Do you protect her because you feel scared or helpless and project those fears on to your child?

The Overprotective Parent assumes she knows what the child needs. Out of love, she regularly anticipates what she believes will be helpful to her child or will make her feel better. She attempts to ward off painful or unpleasant experiences for her child. In her desire to create a "happy" childhood she does not want her child to feel distress, sadness, or to suffer in any way. She means well and hopes to save her child from the inevitable bumps and ruts in the road of life. She may also be trying to avoid re-living her own unhappy childhood experiences. Mothers often say, "When my child hurts, I get a pain in my womb." She truly believes parenting in this way will save her child from stress and trauma.

Symbiosis[23]: Several parenting styles include the dynamic of symbiosis. The Overprotective or Smothering Parent tends to have a particularly strong symbiotic relationship with her daughter.

In a symbiotic relationship, the boundaries between parent and child are so blurred, it is hard to know where one person leaves off and the other begins. The concept is sometimes referred to as Co-dependence,[24] a relationship between two people in which each person is dependent upon and receives reinforcement from the other, whether beneficial or detrimental. It is difficult for the parent or child to know which feelings are her own and which belong to the other person. It is the difference between "This must really hurt," or "I sense you are feeling really sad," which indicates empathy and a sense of the *otherness*, and "Your pain is also my pain," which blurs the distinction of each person. The parent, caught up in a symbiotic relationship, believes her child's needs are the same as hers; her beliefs, attitudes, perceptions, ambitions, and view of the world are the same as the mother, *or should be*. When the parent encounters resistance or rebellion from her child, she can become angry or fearful at the recognition of their separateness as much as the behavior itself. Typically, the child in an overprotective or symbiotic relationship will be very invested in taking care of her mother. She continually tries to meet mother's needs and often neglects her own to do so because she is confused about their separateness.

The Overprotective Parent is usually unaware that her mind-set and actions can seriously hamper the child's development. The earlier children learn age-appropriate coping skills, the more successful they will be as adults. When children learn coping skills at an early age, it becomes an ongoing and natural part of their developmental process. Making mistakes, falling down, and learning how to recover from these events either on their own or with some coaching-- not "helping" from a parent teaches them resilience and the ability to rely on their own resources to get past the difficult times.

The difference between "coaching" and "helping" is the level of involvement. The parent who "helps" her child takes an active role by doing it "for her child." She soothes any hurts or disappointments regularly and can easily overdo it. The child gets the message she is not capable of getting through the experience herself. In "coaching," the parent is very much present, but in a supporting role; she is emotionally available, provides guidance, and encourages the child to come up with her own solutions.

The Smothering Parent overwhelms the child with affection, direction, and interference. She may take over the child's life and will do almost anything to stay in control. She may read her child's diary, e-mails, and text messages. She may listen in on her phone calls and comment on the conversation. She needs to be in constant contact with her child and can even demand reports on every activity, thought, or feeling. In effect, if the parent has her way, the child's life will belong to the mother.

The Overprotective/Smothering Parent usually suffers a lack of security with her own identity. She might have a history of abuse or neglect. If the parent failed to bond with her own parent, she may feel an excessive need to compensate by forging an indelible bond with her child. The dependency is unhealthy for both parties. The child will have a difficult time developing her own individuality. Doing so is likely to threaten her relationship with her mother.

Effects on Child:

Being overprotective sends a message to the child that she is not capable of managing events or feelings. The child lacks trust in her ability to handle the many challenges she faces. What the parent considers "help" can actually handicap the child. The child's self-image is based on how she sees herself through her mother's eyes. The reflection the child sees is a lack of faith in her ability, physically or emotionally, to get through a difficult or not so difficult situation.

The child of an overprotective parent is likely to report how much she was loved and might not be aware of how she felt suffocated or smothered by her parent's love. She may fail to develop physical, emotional, and social skills necessary to function effectively as an adult. She can grow up feeling helpless and dependent on others, with little confidence in her own judgment or ability to get through difficult situations.

Some parents believe they can never be too affectionate; it's a prevalent and desirable form of demonstrating love. Part of the parent's predicament is the fear she's not capable of providing adequate affection. She likely has a great desire to ensure her child is being comforted when she needs it. However, she isn't able to gauge what kind, how much, and when to provide the comfort. Her own parents didn't provide the information she needs.

When my first child was an infant, my neighbor who I respected, said, "Too much affection will spoil your child." So, I held back and later regretted it. Some parents believe you can never give too much affection; your child will let you know when they don't want your attentions. This may be true for some children. Others may not want the affection but are reluctant to let their parent know for fear of displeasing her.

In my therapy practice, I learned some children interpret affection as an attempt to take away their feelings, especially if it is given when the child is upset. With my own children, there were definitely times when I held back because I knew I needed to let them have their feelings; it was very difficult for me. One daughter in particular expressed her need to be alone with her feelings. I longed to comfort her and ease her sadness. On closer examination, I realized I wanted to protect her from her unpleasant feelings *and* save myself from the distress of feeling her pain.

It's helpful to learn to read your child's needs at any given time. It's tough to withhold your urge to comfort or reach out and hug your child when she indicates she doesn't want you to. The way she communicates her needs will vary with each child. If you pay close attention, and with some trial and error experience, you will learn her non-verbal cues. You can also just ask her, "Would you like me to give you a hug now?" Even with this effort, you may not get the *real* answer. Pay attention to her body language to get her unspoken message.

The overprotected child may go along with the parent in an effort to be accepted and loved. She will apologize for any behavior the parent considers unacceptable. If she is uncertain, the child will assume the parent's actions are justified, and therefore she must be wrong. Some children will rebel sooner or later. This can be a healthy response as the child attempts to learn about herself. The more the child rebels or resists, the more insistent or even angry the parent may become. The child who is striving for her own identity will need to be strong, determined, and resilient in order to withstand the conflict and rejection. Some are able to do this, even if it is at the cost of the relationship. Others cave in at some point and regress to a state of dependence and obedience.

Examples:

I. Gwen was surprised at how she felt when she became a mother. Previously, she knew she liked children but didn't necessarily think she was cut out to be a mother. When her daughter was born, she was overwhelmed with the love and maternal instincts that blossomed in her.

She struggled for years to create a healthy balance between indulging in her desire to give her child everything, and setting appropriate boundaries as a parent.

She had to dig deep and learn more about her own motivations for her actions. She learned that part of her attachment to her daughter was fueled by the lack of attachment she felt to her own mother. Gwen wanted to be the kind of mother she never had; her mother was self-absorbed and unable to show any genuine affection. She wanted to compensate for all the years of deprivation she had experienced. When this awareness sunk in, Gwen was able to back off and gradually learn which were her needs and which were her daughter's.

II. Carrie and her mother Dora, a single mother, had a very close relationship. Dora did everything for Carrie, including washing and drying her hair even as Carrie became a teenager. They both loved the ritual-- it made them feel connected and cared for. They created an incubated world of their own with their consuming attention to each other. Neither of them had much of an outside life, preferring each other's company to any other. As a result, Carrie was an outsider at school, didn't make friends, and didn't cultivate outside interests of her own. It wasn't as if she tried and failed at developing a social life, she never attempted it. After all, Dora was there to meet all of her needs.

There were some significant dilemmas for Carrie and Dora. If either of them had any thoughts of forming another relationship, it would mean devastation to the other. And, what would happen to Carrie when Dora died? As it evolved, Carrie became very depressed as she reached her twenties with many of her normal developmental needs not met. She began acting out by becoming sexually promiscuous which further increased her depression. She felt incapable of forming any close relationships with men or women. Dora felt helpless as she watched her daughter struggle, which caused her to distance herself from Carrie. The tightly woven fabric of their relationship began to unravel. Fortunately for Carrie, she reached out and started therapy.

She gradually learned who she was and with tremendous internal conflict, began to separate from Dora. During this process, Carrie became very angry and was unable to show any compassion for her mother. At this point Dora could have really benefited from therapy as well, but declined to do so. They became estranged; Dora developed physical ailments, and ended up in a nursing home.

This is a true account of a severe example of an Overprotective Parent. Most overprotective parents don't go to this extreme but still hinder the child's normal development and ability to acquire necessary coping skills to help navigate life.

III. Elsie and her mother Frieda were very loving with each other. They delighted in every word, every expression they shared. Even as Elsie grew from infant, to toddler, to child, she felt inseparable from her mother. If her mother left the house for any reason, Elsie would experience severe anxiety. When Frieda returned, Elsie clung to her and couldn't let go. Frieda was flattered and responded with the reward of affection. She bought them matching outfits, which they always wore when they were out in public. Many observers thought it was "cute" and some were even envious of the close relationship. This continued until puberty when Elsie felt a need to find out who she was apart from her mother. Frieda did nothing to encourage her daughter to make friends. When Elsie's mother started reading her e-mails and text messages, Elsie became furious. She was clearly ready to separate and her mother took that as the ultimate rejection.

The more Elsie resisted the interference, the more determined her mother was to be involved in her life. Frieda tried playing the victim to elicit sympathy and compliance. When that didn't work, she sought other ways to connect with Elsie: she ordered the same foods in restaurants, developed the same hobbies, and dressed like Elsie. Their roles essentially became reversed. As a result, Elsie spent as little time with her mother as possible and used anger as a distancing mechanism.

Going off to college became Elsie's escape, her first sense of real freedom. As she learned to become her own person, she was able to let go of most of her anger and began to feel sorry for her mother. Their relationship became more cordial although Elsie felt like she had to continually be on guard for signs of interference. Since Frieda was never able to find her own life and interests, their relationship was strained, and the closeness that felt like a bond when Elsie was young, was gone.

Helpful Hints:

It's a challenge to know where to draw the line between appropriate interest and attentiveness, or protection that becomes a handicap. Here are some questions you can ask yourself. They can be difficult to answer. Take your time to think about these before answering.

- "Am I doing this for my child to make her feel better, or to make me feel better?"

- "What does my child need more right now, my "help" or the tools to learn how to figure things out on her own.
- "How much do I truly want her to become self-sufficient?"
- "How much do I enjoy having her be dependent on me?"
- "What needs of my own am I trying to meet by encouraging dependence?"
- "What might be the advantages for each of us in her becoming more independent?"

The bottom line is to pay attention to your child's reaction to your display of affection or help. Whether the child is in a good mood or upset, she will likely give you some signals as to how receptive she is. The clues will be overt or subtle. It's important to focus on the subtle signs, such as lack of response, discomfort in her body language, or behaviors such as squirming, making faces, diverting your attention, withdrawing, etc.

A phrase I learned many years ago was very helpful to me in determining when to hold on and when to let go: "Do nothing regularly for your child that she can do for herself."

Overprotective Parenting Scale:

Mother	1	2	3	4	5	6	7	8	9	10
Father	1	2	3	4	5	6	7	8	9	10
Spouse	1	2	3	4	5	6	7	8	9	10
Me	1	2	3	4	5	6	7	8	9	10

Smothering Parenting Scale:

Mother	1	2	3	4	5	6	7	8	9	10
Father	1	2	3	4	5	6	7	8	9	10
Spouse	1	2	3	4	5	6	7	8	9	10
Me	1	2	3	4	5	6	7	8	9	10

THE NURTURING PARENT

Description:

The Nurturing Parent is able to demonstrate caring, empathy, and support in appropriate doses. She does not take on unwarranted responsibility for her child's feelings or actions. Her motto is: *I'm here to guide my child into self-sufficiency.*

The challenge for the nurturing parent is to provide effective caring without slipping into being over-protective, as discussed in the previous section. It means finding ways to appropriately demonstrate your powerful feelings of love while remaining aware of the effects of your actions on your child. As a parent, you want to ensure your child has a tangible experience of the depth and durability of your love without feeling overwhelmed or smothered. *The way you communicate* that experience will strongly influence how your child receives and makes sense of your actions.

Effects on Child:

If your child is receiving appropriate nurturing, she will demonstrate self-confidence; resilience, a sense of responsibility, a willingness to try things on her own, and genuine appreciation for your guidance.

The following are some examples that demonstrate your efforts to nurture are *not* having the desired effect:

Your child will let you know your attempts at nurturing are not successful if she stiffens up when you try to be affectionate; if she wriggles out of your grasp; if she makes a joke in an attempt to divert your attention or to disguise her discomfort; if she gets angry or tries other distractions; if she tunes you out; if she verbally or non-verbally communicates *she* wants to take care of *you.*

Your child's expression of discomfort will vary, depending on her personality and her age. Her response may also be a reaction to earlier events or experiences that make her feel uncomfortable with your attempts at nurturing. This may or may not have anything to do with you. It could be related to her experiences with other people. It could also be related to the particular mood or state of mind she is in at the moment. In any event, she will send signals that let you know to hold off or pull back. It's important to pay close attention so you can better understand what is happening.

It's also helpful to keep in mind Erikson's stages of child development as outlined in Chapter 3.[8] Many of us know first-hand or have heard about children who start to reject attempts at affection from a parent when they enter the puberty or pre-adolescent phase. This is not a rejection of your love; it is the beginning of her need to discover who she is as a separate individual, and to take her first steps towards self-sufficiency. This is a positive sign, no matter how much you as the parent feel the first pangs of "losing" your child. Your child's actions signal it is time for *your development* to shift, to move from the initial stage of love, comfort, and cuddling to the gradual process of letting go.

One parent described to me the surprise and confusion she felt when she tried to put her arms around her daughter to comfort her about a recent event and was pushed away. The fifteen year-old daughter said to her mother, "Mom, I need to learn about my own feelings and how to deal with them."

Not many daughters (or sons) would be able to express themselves this well. They are more likely to react to some of the ways described above that let you know you are missing the cues.

As a nurturing parent, you need to continually work towards clarity for yourself:

- To what extent do you truly put your child's needs first?
- To what extent is your nurturing behavior an attempt to fulfill your own unmet nurturing needs?
- How well are you able to tolerate your child's discomfort?

It is unrealistic to assume you as a parent can consistently meet your child's needs. It is equally unreasonable to always recognize when you hope to get your own needs met through your nurturing behavior.

Not reaching your goal does not mean you are not a good enough parent. Asking yourself the questions does mean you are committed to being honest and truthful with yourself. Your self-reflection improves the quality of your parenting and becomes a valuable model for your child. When you admit your needs to yourself you will be able to say to your child, "This doesn't seem to be helping you, maybe I'm paying more attention to my needs rather than yours, and that isn't fair to you."

Examples:

I. Isabel was determined to be a nurturing mother, especially since her own mother was not. When Debra was born, Isabel was thrilled to have the opportunity to lavish the affection she was denied on her daughter. Things were fine for a while, until Debra was about six. Isabel noticed her daughter stiffened up or pulled away when she put her arms around her. This was Isabelle's first sign her nurturing gesture was not what Debra wanted or needed.

As Debra grew older, she ran to her room when she was upset and refused to tell her mother what was wrong. At first, Isabel felt confused, hurt, and rejected. Fortunately Isabel was eventually able to put her own feelings aside and focus on what her daughter was communicating. She realized she was trying to give her daughter what she missed in her own childhood rather than seeing Debra as a unique individual whose needs were different. Isabel learned that what her daughter really wanted was time to process her own feelings and then come to her mother to talk about what was upsetting her. They both learned to communicate more clearly what helped and what didn't. It required Isabel to fine tune her listening skills and to acknowledge she couldn't heal her own pain through her daughter.

II. Sharon's parents were good role models for her. They seemed generally tuned in to what their daughter needed, which would vary depending on the situation. When Sharon became a mother, she had a healthy respect for her daughter Allison's moods and what she could do to help. Up to the age of six, Sharon recognized her daughter needed help identifying and describing her feelings, so one of her main nurturing activities was to help her find words for her emotions.

From the time Allison turned six, Sharon recognized that sometimes nurturing meant leaving Allison alone to work a problem out herself. Other times it meant suggesting they sit down and talk about what was bothering her. And in other situations it meant an educated guess that what Allison told her she wanted wasn't really what she wanted. For example, she was able to translate Allison's statement, "I can do it myself," expressed in a defiant voice. Sharon picked up the fear and anxiety in her daughter's tone and responded with, "If it were me, this would be pretty scary. I'm here to help you if you want it."

Helpful Hints:

How can you know what is the right amount of nurturing? One of the most reliable sources of information is your child. When you pay close attention to how your child responds to your "nurturing," in as objective a way as you can manage, she will let you know verbally or non-verbally what is best for her. You need to learn her lack of response is not personal, it is the best way she knows how to cope with her own feelings in the moment.

What do you hope will be the result of your nurturing? Reflect on the following questions. Your initial response will likely indicate your conscious motivations. You may need to dig deeper to uncover any subconscious reasons:

1. Do you primarily hope she will feel supported and safe?

2. Do you primarily hope she will gain strength to face her challenges?
3. Do you hope she will appreciate and love you most for your guidance and support?
4. Do you hope she will be nurturing to you, directly or indirectly, in response?

The first two questions are in your child's best interests. The last two are about meeting your needs. Which are the most important to you, and would you still willingly provide the nurturing if you didn't get the third or fourth response?

Nurturing Parenting Scale:

Mother	1	2	3	4	5	6	7	8	9	10
Father	1	2	3	4	5	6	7	8	9	10
Spouse	1	2	3	4	5	6	7	8	9	10
Me	1	2	3	4	5	6	7	8	9	10

Note: If you rate yourself very high on this scale, it could indicate that your nurturing crosses the line between healthy nurturing and being overprotective.

One way to evaluate this is to compare your responses on this scale to the one on the Overprotective Parent Scale. Notice the ratings you give for your own mother and/or father and how you feel about their nurturing. It may give you some added perspective.

THE OVERACHIEVING PARENT

Description:

The Overachieving Parent sets and pushes goals or activities for her child mainly shaped by the parent's own needs, wishes, or interests. She can be kind, demanding, or a benevolent dictator. Her fantasy is to have her child live out her own unfulfilled dreams. If Mom wanted to be a star athlete, actress, a doctor or lawyer, she may look for signs of interest in her daughter in those areas. She will even erroneously interpret signs, so intent is she to have her daughter satisfy her own desires. She will justify the selected pursuit as "good" for her daughter and prod her into action.

There's also the parent who has made substantial achievements, whether in work, sports, or community, and wants her daughter to follow in her footsteps. She sees it as an opportunity to forge a stronger bond with her child. The problem is it's based on the parent's needs with little consideration for her daughter's interests.

The Overachieving Parent can also try to recruit her child by "getting on the bandwagon and then leading it." A child can show an interest in an activity, and while the appeal may be mild or moderate, the parent jumps in and takes over, assuming this is the child's passion or life calling. The attraction may be a passing one, but the parent doesn't see it that way, especially if it fits into her own dreams, or the desire for her child to "shine" in some area. The parent has difficulty going along with the ebb and flow of the child's developmental process.

Effects on Child:

The child of an Overachieving Parent will either go along with the parent's pressure in an effort to gain approval, or she will rebel, which can take several forms. One way this comes out is outright defiance and refusal to follow the parent's wishes. In other instances, the child may act out her lack of interest indirectly. For example, she becomes so absorbed in another activity it precludes participation in what the parent wants. She may take part in the activity but either goofs off, won't cooperate, acts resentful, or simply fails. The child may also manifest problems in other areas: she may pick on siblings, have problems with other children, or develop physical symptoms. These all serve to derail the parent from pursuing her agenda. If the child's response is indirect, the parent is not likely to recognize it as a cry for help. Usually the truth doesn't surface unless the parent can pick up the signals and respond appropriately. Whatever the cause these behaviors signal concern and need your attention.

The child who goes along with the parent's demands may or may not be interested, but often acts as if she is. She may not even know herself whether or not she truly cares because she feels a strong need to please her parent. Newly minted adults have been known to pursue careers for many years, well into middle-age, all because they followed a parent's implied or explicit wishes. Then they wake up one morning and realize they hate their work.

Examples:

I. Danya's mother Pearl is a successful businesswoman, who is ambitious both for herself and her daughter. Pearl enjoys the financial rewards and ego gratification that comes from her accomplishments and wants the same for Danya. However, Danya's interests are in creative expression. She loves to write and draw, and at thirteen, has little interest in following in her mother's footsteps. As a result, there is considerable friction between the two.

Pearl continually tries to convince her daughter there will be plenty of time to pursue her creative interests once she becomes successful and can write her own ticket. She shows little understanding of the passion Danya has for her creativity, despite efforts to explain to her mother how important it is to her. Recently, Danya's grades in school have begun to drop, and she has little concern about improving them. Pearl has hired a tutor and continually tells Danya she will never get into a good college if she doesn't bring her grades up.

Even though Pearl is highly intelligent, she doesn't recognize the message her daughter is sending. Danya herself isn't consciously aware, she just feels unmotivated. The harder Pearl tries, the more Danya sabotages her efforts. She "forgets" her tutoring appointments, leaves her homework at school, and gets sick often. The pattern encourages Danya to fail.

II. Leslie loves being a mom, but regrets never having pursued a career. She had a dream of becoming an opera star and gave it up for her priority of marriage and family. Leslie's daughter Sara, now ten, loves math and computers, and aspires to pursue technology as a career path. Leslie has been trying to get Sara interested in music and the arts, hoping *someone in the family* will live out her dream.

She tells Sara the field she is interested in is dominated by men and Sara won't have much of a chance to succeed. She continually plays classical music at home, even when Sara is trying to study and tells her mom it is distracting. Sara feels unsupported and judged for her choices. Leslie at times does give tacit encouragement, but her message is clear: Sara won't be able to please her mother unless she follows a musical career.

Helpful Hints:

In both of the above instances, the mothers are not harsh or mean—they are just focused on their own desires. Their own agendas blind them to the harm they are doing to their relationship with their daughters.

How much attention are you paying to the relationship you truly want to build with your daughter? When you want to develop or improve a relationship, the tendency is to look for the similarities and ignore the differences, believing that's what will strengthen the relationship.

Do you mistakenly believe the close relationship you desire will come from having common interests? It's a challenge to be able to put aside your own hopes and dreams and allow yourself to mentally and emotionally enter into your daughter's world.

Spend some time reflecting on your unrealized hopes and dreams. To what extent do you feel sad, regretful, resentful or frustrated about not pursuing your dreams? If you feel it is important for your child to follow in your footsteps, what are your reasons—the *real* ones? They might be a need to be validated for your choices, wanting to make your bond with your child stronger, or something related to your own childhood.

To develop more objectivity, pay attention to your feelings and what's behind your attitudes and actions. Notice your child's responses. Does she seem truly enthusiastic? Does she seem to want to please you? What have you noticed about your daughter's own interests and inclinations? How do they differ from yours?

Overachieving Parenting Scale:

Mother	1	2	3	4	5	6	7	8	9	10
Father	1	2	3	4	5	6	7	8	9	10
Spouse	1	2	3	4	5	6	7	8	9	10
Me	1	2	3	4	5	6	7	8	9	10

THE HELPLESS OR DEPENDENT PARENT

Description:

The Helpless Parent seems unable to manage household, spouse, children, and life. She may express her helplessness by manipulating others, or simply by doing nothing. She will say things like, "I just don't know how to do this, could you please do it for me?" She might say, "You are so much better/smarter at doing this; would you please take care of it?" The parent may spend her time watching TV, reading, engage in passive activities or find multiple reasons for not being at home. She could be out shopping, lunching with friends, or just taking off for a long drive. She could also be someone who hides behind an alcohol or drug habit.

The Helpless Parent may also be, or appear to be, easily overwhelmed by life's events, such as financial problems, loss of a job, divorce, illness, accident, death of her spouse or of a family member or friend. She may even show a lack of ability to handle everyday issues, such as an appliance that breaks down, paying bills, following through with plans, or making scheduled doctor's appointments.

Effects on Child:

The child often sees the distress of the parent and feels a need to jump in and take care of her. Her action comes not only from compassion, but also the child's need to return her mother to a more functional state so she can carry out her parenting duties. Her goal is to restore the balance and become the child again. The Helpless Parent may or may not care. The daughter's nurturing can be genuine as well as a form of manipulation.

The child might emulate the parent and adopt her behaviors or become the "helper" who takes up the slack by doing the chores and even becomes a surrogate parent to her siblings. She may carry resentment for not having a parent who is there to guide and nurture her in the ways she needs. Even if she receives personal gratification and a sense of self-sufficiency, it comes at a price to her. Depression or anger towards herself or the person she is helping is a likely result.

If the child becomes the "helper," she develops skills she can use as an adult. She feels rewarded and enjoys a competency she may find useful in other experiences. The child who turns into a caretaker as compensation, as a learned behavior, or as an attempt to find validation and an identity will encounter challenges later in life. It will be difficult to set boundaries, maintain a clear perspective on her priorities or harbor a fear that without this role she has little or no value in the world. As she gets burned out, she may also eventually turn into the same helpless parent she's been trying to avoid.

Examples:

I. As a result of being overprotected and not having the opportunity to develop coping and life management skills, Kelly has always felt incapable of handling life. As soon as her daughter Patty was old enough, around age five, Kelly started asking her to "help" out around the house. Initially, Patty was delighted to do anything to feel appreciated by her mother. She also felt a sense of power and proficiency. Patty received many compliments from friends and neighbors.

As Patty approached her teen years, she started to feel she had missed out on her childhood, and began to resent her mother. At this point she started to rebel and became less cooperative in going along with her mother's requests for help. This frustrated Kelly, and she complained and berated Patty for not caring about her.

Needless to say, their relationship deteriorated. Kelly became even more helpless in a desperate attempt to get Patty back into her old role. It created a vicious cycle, and escalated to the point of estrangement between mother and daughter by the time Patty was eighteen.

II. Brenda learned early in life that she was good at getting other people to do things for her. She enjoyed the attention and the feeling of power it gave her. It was like a game for her, and became a way of life. When Brenda's daughter Charlotte was born, her parenting style evolved out of this habit. Brenda didn't actually feel helpless because she was pulling the strings. Acting helpless was the introduction to the game. Brenda was not fully conscious of her actions; they had become an ingrained habit.

When Charlotte was young, like Patty she willingly accepted her role. As she grew older, she realized it was a game, and even tried to call her mother on it. By this time, Brenda had honed her skills to an art form, and had the means to derail Charlotte's efforts. She would act indignant when Charlotte accused her of playing the "game," and if necessary, would get emotional and cry or play "poor me." She would say things like:" "I've tried so hard to be a good mother and teach you what's right, and this is what I get?" She made no effort to take responsibility for her actions. By the time Charlotte was in her teens, she simply opted out of the game and as soon as she was out of high school, moved out.

Helpful Hints:

Whether this style evolved by upbringing or design, it will eventually backfire. You not only do your daughter a disservice, you do harm to yourself. You limit your own development and deny yourself opportunities to realize your own natural talents and abilities.

You may feel truly helpless as a result of a belief you developed early in life. Very few mothers are in fact helpless unless there is a serious psychological or physical reason. Even women who are physically disabled have learned to become competent and independent and to make valuable contributions to their families and their communities.

If you see yourself in this description: pay close attention to how this behavior makes you feel. Chances are, while temporarily satisfying; it will not make you feel good about yourself. Seek out ways to develop new interests and skills that will help you feel more mentally, physically, and emotionally competent. You can take classes, read books, or use the assistance of a coach or therapist if needed.

Helpless or Dependent Parenting Scale:

Mother	1	2	3	4	5	6	7	8	9	10
Father	1	2	3	4	5	6	7	8	9	10
Spouse	1	2	3	4	5	6	7	8	9	10
Me	1	2	3	4	5	6	7	8	9	10

THE CONTROLLING PARENT

Description:

The Controlling Parent engages in direct or indirect manipulation of the child's thoughts, feelings, and/or behavior to get the child to conform to the parent's wishes. Arbitrary conditions or demands are made on the child that are often puzzling. She can't make sense of her parent's actions. Little sensitivity is shown to the child's responses or needs.

As a result, the child becomes confused about what is appropriate. The parent can be stern or kind. The stern parent will look and act more like a drill sergeant or a tough corporate CEO. The kind parent will present an appearance of helpfulness, *so* helpful they end up doing the child's schoolwork, art project or other activity for them, to show them how to do it right. An example might be: If the child is involved in a sports activity, the controlling parent will be on the sidelines (or on the field) continually shouting directions to the child.

There are myriad ways parents can be controlling. Most of the Parenting Styles described in this book involve efforts to control the child. Some examples of control in different styles: the Helpless Parent controls by getting her child to do what she doesn't want to do herself or finds ways for the child to feel sorry for her. The Laissez-Faire Parent (discussed later) also controls by getting the child to fend for herself. The difference between the two is the Helpless Parent sends a "poor me" message, and the Laissez-Faire parent sends an "I don't care what you do" message.

Since the child relies on her parent for survival, any given Parenting Style is bound to influence her reactions and behaviors. The daughter's response will depend on what she perceives will make her safe.

Effects on Child:

With an overtly controlling parent, the child learns she can't be trusted to figure things out on her own. The messages to her is, "you can't do it right, well-enough, or good enough to please me." The child struggles to discover her own capabilities. She usually suffers a lack of confidence and becomes fearful and anxious, not knowing what to do. She believes she is bound to fall short. Some of her responses include becoming rebellious and refusing to go along with the parent's demands, since she will never figure it out anyhow. Even attempts to cooperate can make her feel inadequate when the parent jumps in to "help." The parent's typical response is a renewed effort to amp up the control. A vicious cycle is created that can easily escalate both the parent's and child's dysfunctional behavior.

The following examples where at least one parent is controlling provide insight into the dynamics of this style. Often the child will modify some of her behaviors. Her perception of threats to her safety will determine what actions she takes. She may try very hard to please her parent and becomes nervous even as she makes her efforts. She may become passive, inept, or uncaring, subtle forms of rebellion. The severity of the threat to the child will determine the strength of her reaction. The extreme examples more clearly illustrate how this style affects the well-being of the child and her relationship with her mother.

Examples:

I. Tessa came from a family that was rigid and strict, with a set of rules for everything. When her daughter Libby was born, Tessa felt very nervous about whether she knew enough to be a good mother. She compensated by emulating her own experience, and set very stringent standards for Libby's care as an infant and later for her behavior as she was growing up. Libby was put on a tight feeding and sleeping schedule with little flexibility. This schedule was adhered to, even when it didn't conform to Libby's hunger cries. The schedule came first even when it created inconvenience for the family such as turning down invitations to events with family and friends. As a toddler, Libby learned to make sure her toys were all put away on their designated shelves. If she was slow at picking up her toys or didn't put them where they belonged, Tessa would stand over her and insist she conform to her demands. When Libby was in school, she was not allowed to defer from her homework routine for *any* reason.

There were constant punishments given out for infringements of the "routine." Libby became a nervous and fearful child; she was never quite sure of what was expected. It seemed there were always new rules being made. Her behavior became compulsive in an effort to produce some predictability, which created problems for Libby at school. She would get upset if the schedule was changed or even if her classmates didn't do assignments exactly as directed. Even though she was a bright child, she had trouble making friends. Libby's parents were often called in for meetings with the teachers who were at a loss about what to do. Her parents didn't recognize how they were contributing to the problem, so Libby was labeled a "difficult" child.

II. Adele came from a family quite opposite to Tessa's. Her family was so loose, there were no rules, no suggested ways of doing things, no guidance whatsoever. Even her house was in a constant state of disarray; it was impossible to find anything. Adele felt at such loose ends that when she became a mother she was determined to create a sense of order instead of the chaos she grew up with.

Adele overcompensated for her experience by creating a household much like Tessa's. Instead of becoming nervous and anxious, Adele's daughter Sally rebelled. She purposely kept her room in a mess, disobeying the "rules." She shouted at her mother for being too uptight. There was constant friction between Adele and Sally. Both felt out of control and helpless to figure out a way to make things better. They tolerated each other but were unable to form any meaningful connection.

Helpful Hints:

Even as you believe you have your child's best interests at heart, take time to go a little deeper into understanding yourself. Who in your life has shown signs of controlling behaviors? How did you feel about those behaviors and the person who carried them out?

Read the information on Control in Chapter 8 and take the assessment quiz in the appendix at the end of the book. In what ways do you feel out of control internally and compensate for those feelings by trying to control others?

Controlling Parenting Scale:

Mother	1	2	3	4	5	6	7	8	9	10
Father	1	2	3	4	5	6	7	8	9	10
Spouse	1	2	3	4	5	6	7	8	9	10
Me	1	2	3	4	5	6	7	8	9	10

THE ENCOURAGING PARENT

Description:

The Encouraging Parent allows and fosters expression of her child's feelings, ideas, and dreams. She maintains an interested, accepting and non-interfering attitude. She demonstrates support and caring, much like the nurturing parent. This parent is likely to say, "I believe you can achieve anything you want to. It is likely to take effort, and you will make mistakes, and I will be there cheering you on all the way."

A parent who is willing and able to see her child as a separate individual even at a young age is an important factor. This seems to contradict the concept of bonding, which is essential for the parent/child relationship to flourish. It's important to be clear on what the purpose of the bonding process is, and how to cultivate it in a healthy and functional way. The parent needs to draw clear lines between over-identification and appropriate bonding and to be true to those boundaries.

The purpose of healthy bonding in a parent/child relationship for you is to feel sufficiently connected to your child so you can provide all the care and guidance necessary for her to grow and develop into a healthy adult. For your child, the bonding process allows her to feel safe, supported and cared for while she navigates the road to independence. Beneficial bonding involves trust, relatedness and commitment.

All humans possess language, emotions, and behaviors; the tools of connection that enable you to guide your child on the path to maturity. Even in animal life, a healthy bonding connection can occur without the use of spoken language as we know it. This underscores the role of non-verbal language in our communications.

The model we see in nature validates the importance of the bonding experience. If you observe the animal world, you will notice how the parent teaches her offspring to become self-sufficient as early as possible. The challenge you face is to recognize when and to what extent the physical and emotional ties of the bond need to be loosened. If you have successfully progressed through Erikson's stages[8] and reached the Generativity phase (Chapter 3), you will be able to relinquish your own needs for the sake of our child. You will be ready to let go, even if it is accompanied by more than a few twinges of pain or tears. The purpose of the bonding process is to help your child get a foothold in the world. *She is carried only until she can walk.* If you learn to let go of the need to "carry" her through each stage She will learn to walk on her own, and later, to stand on her own two feet physically, mentally and emotionally.

Effects on Child:

The child of an Encouraging Parent will feel more competent, and willing to try new things. She will feel more supported and understood, and experience less external pressure to achieve. She will be able to focus on her own true interests and feel the freedom to pursue those interests.

If the parent overdoes the encouragement, the child may feel some pressure. This can happen when a parent notices a child's interest in an activity, and becomes more enthusiastic than her child. It can also happen if the parent fails to notice when the child is losing interest in an activity for any reason. It is helpful to check in with your child periodically to get some feedback from her.

Examples:

I. Sylvia's main goal in life was to be the shining example of a positive influence on her daughter. She delved into books, parenting classes, and lectures on effective parenting.

One of the principles she learned was that of encouragement. *The child who is encouraged to explore and experiment will have the best chance of developing a strong sense of self (Erikson)[8]*. She will learn by trial and error, and her lessons will help her become clear and focused on what she wants to do with her life. What Sylvia didn't realize was how her immense love for her daughter Annie would compromise the accomplishment of those goals.

The plan worked well when Annie was an infant and toddler. Sylvia provided her daughter with a variety of toys and activities that prompted her to experiment with her body through movement and exercise, and with her mind to explore colors, shapes, and concepts suitable to her stage of development. When Annie was six and wanted to learn how to ride a two-wheeled bicycle, Sylvia bought her a bike and proceeded to teach her the basics of steering and balancing. This was the fork in the road when Sylvia's love turned into overprotection.

When Annie got on her new bike, Sylvia had a hard time letting her daughter wobble and fall. She helped Annie up after the first fall, and then began holding on to the handlebars to help her steer and balance, a natural reaction. The problem was Sylvia couldn't seem to let go at the appropriate time. The unspoken message to Annie was: "I don't trust you to get the hang of this on your own. You need me to be there to guide you until you get it just right." No more wobbling or falls for Annie. Her experimenting days came to a halt. Annie became increasingly frustrated, and eventually refused to "learn" to ride her bike. In time, she did go on to learn to ride her bike when she was twelve, her friends were all riding and Mom wasn't around to watch.

II. MaryAnn's mother, Sybil, went back and forth between her desire to protect and her goal to help her daughter become self-sufficient. Fortunately she was acutely aware of the struggle within herself. Sybil was able to strike a balance most of the time. She did slip up occasionally. MaryAnn was exposed to several different activities, and Sybil watched to see what types of experiences her daughter gravitated towards. She made it clear to MaryAnn that she could choose whatever activities she wanted.

MaryAnn's first attempts at bike riding were frustrating, and she told her mother she didn't want to learn to ride, even though most of her friends were already riding. Sybil's response was, "That's okay; you don't need to learn now. You just let me know if a time comes when you feel ready." MaryAnn was quite relieved, and turned her attention to reading which her mother encouraged. Sybil allowed MaryAnn to pick up or drop activities at her own pace, realizing her daughter was progressing through developmental stages, not strictly determined by her age or what her peers were doing.

MaryAnn showed a real talent for the piano, picking up tunes and playing them by ear. Sybil asked her if she wanted lessons, and MaryAnn said, "Yes". She took lessons for about a year, and seemed to enjoy them. One day MaryAnn said to her mother, "I don't want to take lessons anymore." This was tough for Sybil; she saw the real talent her daughter had and hated to see it go to waste. In addition, Sybil had always wanted to play the piano and never had lessons. She hoped MaryAnn would live out her dream.

However, Sybil was committed to her promise to herself not to push her daughter. She engaged MaryAnn in a supportive discussion: "I'm wondering what feelings you are having about your piano lessons." MaryAnn's response was, "It's just getting too hard for me—I'd rather take drawing lessons." At this point Sybil could have given her daughter a lecture on "quitting" and how lots of things in life are difficult. She decided against that approach because she sensed it wouldn't be helpful. With great restraint, Sybil said, "Okay! If you ever want to go back to it, just let me know." Growing up, MaryAnn never did go back to her lessons. When she was an adult and living on her own, she bought a keyboard and started to play on her own schedule. She told her mother, "If you had pushed me to continue my lessons, I think I never would have gone back to playing."

Helpful Hints:

In the case of Sylvia and Annie, was the experience of learning to ride a bike a developmental issue as Sylvia reasoned, or could she have done something different? What if the skill in question was not related to a physical activity? Sylvia came to realize while she encouraged Annie to read books of her own choosing, schoolwork assignments came back with less than perfect scores. Sylvia became anxious and began to "coach" Annie on how to find the right answers, and did the research with her. She proofread her papers and edited them.

How much harm was actually done? This is a difficult question to answer. What might you have done differently? What are the clues you can detect to shed light on the difference between encouragement, overprotection or lack of support?

As always, it is valuable to pay attention to your child's non-verbal signals. Ask yourself if your child's interest or activity is something you enjoy or wish you had pursued. Your encouragement may be influenced by something other than an objective perspective.

When your own wishes and dreams are reflected in your actions toward your child, it will come across with a level of tension, however subtle. Your child will pick up on this and react, even at a subliminal level. True encouragement based on an objective recognition of who your child is requires you to put your ego needs on the shelf—in the closet, far enough away from the temptation to bring them out.

From another perspective, if you have no interest in what your child wants to do, you run the risk of subtly discouraging her. You also need to pay attention to your lack of support and make sure you stay objective. A child can have an interest in an activity and still feel intimidated, reluctant to make a first attempt. When you pay attention, you can pick up those signals and find ways to help her get past her fears. Ask her what she likes about the activity. Then ask her what makes her feel hesitant. Depending on her response, you can suggest she give it a try and see what happens. You can let her know you will be by her side to guide her. Encouragement is important to help guide your child past her fears and to allow her to experiment with new activities.

When you or your child is actively engaged in activities that provide a form of personal gratification, independent of anyone else's participation, each of you will have a healthy means to reinforce your self-worth. If the activity you encourage in your child is something you have always wanted to do, consider taking it up for yourself! Some other ways to find your own personal fulfillment could be to pursue a creative or physical activity that you enjoy for the pure pleasure of doing. It could be giving back to your community without any thought of reward. It could be taking classes or even working towards a college degree. Pursuing your own interests can help avoid projecting your needs onto your child.

Encouraging Parenting Scale:

Mother	1	2	3	4	5	6	7	8	9	10
Father	1	2	3	4	5	6	7	8	9	10
Spouse	1	2	3	4	5	6	7	8	9	10
Me	1	2	3	4	5	6	7	8	9	10

THE DEFENSIVE PARENT

Description:

The Defensive Parent continually excuses, justifies, or rationalizes her actions. She takes the position of always being "right" and rarely, if ever, apologizes. She is unwilling to take responsibility-- to see the error of her ways. She will invariably pass the blame onto someone else, or will rationalize her behavior to make it seem acceptable. She may accuse her spouse, child, or whoever else is in the conversation of the very behavior she exhibits.

For example, if she overreacts to a situation and her spouse speaks up and tells her to calm down, she will likely turn to him and say, "You are overreacting." This is called *projection,* a defense mechanism that causes her to accuse someone else of what she is doing. It's a way to avoid the pain of unacceptable conduct. She denies to herself and others that her actions could be hurtful to those she cares about.

Effects on Child:

The child who lives with a Defensive Parent will soon learn everything is her fault. She may accept the blame or fight against it. If she accepts it, she will do so actively or passively. In the active response, she is so eager to please her parent that she will immediately step up to take responsibility, hoping this will bring her the assurances of the love and acceptance she craves. If her response is passive acceptance, she will give in to the parent in order to keep the peace and good will. She may long to stand up for herself, knowing instinctively she is not at fault, but is afraid. Her response will not have the ring of sincerity to satisfy her parent, often resulting in further repercussions.

The child who fights against an accusation will find herself in a losing battle. Her parent will stand firm and may escalate the finger-pointing, adding additional charges to the original one. The longer and harder the child fights for her rights, the more the volume gets turned up, until one or the other storms out of the room (or house) or gives up out of sheer exhaustion.

This child can grow up attempting to compensate for her inferiority by becoming like her defensive parent, or she may choose a mate that will be just like her parent, while she repeats her childhood role, and the cycle will be perpetuated. In either case, the child grows up with a flawed self-image.

Examples:

I. Eleanor grew up with a mother who was never wrong. When they disagreed, it meant Eleanor could never be right. In order to protect her sense of self, she developed the habit of finding reasons for her behavior, continually making excuses or apologizing. As Eleanor grew up, she carried this practice with her into her relationships with friends, teachers, boyfriends, her husband, and eventually her own children. While these people may not have been critical of her, she was hyper-vigilant, and read her own meaning into words, facial expressions and body language, anticipating a negative reaction even when none was forthcoming. Her sense of self-worth had suffered a severe blow.

When she became a parent, Eleanor was very sensitive to the reactions of her children. Despite her vow not to repeat the conditions under which she was raised, she would often get defensive. When her daughter Adelaide would get angry at her, Eleanor would either lash out at her to justify her own actions, give Adelaide a lecture on what *she* was doing wrong, or retreat with hurt feelings. Eleanor was unable to get out of her own way and attend to her child's needs.

Adelaide took her mother's reactions to mean she had done something wrong even when she was simply expressing her feelings about an event. Adelaide's expressions of feelings were taken as a personal affront to Eleanor. Their communication remained troubled throughout Adelaide's childhood. They grew apart, and when Adelaide became an adult, their infrequent times together became a shouting match as Adelaide released long pent-up feelings of frustration and hurt.

II. Claire grew up with a defensive parent. Her mother Elise, lacked the confidence to stand behind her decisions in raising her daughter. These feelings of inadequacy caused Elise to be inconsistent in her actions. She made excuses for her choices, over-explained or reversed her decisions. At times she would get angry and say, "Just do what I say!" or "You don't know what you are talking about."

Claire regularly got mixed messages, and didn't know what to believe. She would alternately experience confusion or feel the need to figure things out herself. Claire gradually lost respect for her mother and turned to friends or other adults for guidance. As an adult, she eventually learned to feel sorry for her mother, and their roles became reversed. Claire limited the amount of time she spent with her mother and she gave up the fantasy of being able to have a free exchange of thoughts and feelings. Claire felt the loss of her mother as a role model throughout her life.

Helpful Hints:

Defensiveness is a human response to threats in our environment. It helps to understand what the triggers are for you. For example, one of the most common defense reactions for many people occurs in response to criticism, real or perceived. It is possible to hear criticism in an innocent comment or question. It will evoke a stronger or weaker reaction depending on whether or not the message was one you heard growing up. It also depends on to what extent you sense an uncomfortable truth in the remarks. If you interpret the comment as evidence you are unlovable or unlikable, your defensive reaction will be stronger. Some people attempt to defuse a negative statement by outwardly agreeing with it even if they inwardly don't. They do this to avoid an argument or other unpleasant consequences.

One helpful response is to check out the speaker's intent. You can say, "Can you tell me if you intended your words/question to be negative (or critical)?" The response you receive will help you put things in perspective. It might even open up an opportunity for dialogue.

Learn to acknowledge at least to yourself whatever truth there is in the comments, without needing to agree with the whole statement. It's important to know what your vulnerable areas are and be willing to respond in a non-defensive way. This is no easy task. It requires you to take a step back (or two) and look at the situation as if you were an objective observer. The more honest you can be with yourself about your shortcomings without judging yourself as unworthy or unlovable, the more you will be able to modify your defensive response.

There are two other factors that influence how you receive negative comments. One depends on the person who is saying them. The other has to do with how the words are spoken. If you know the person to be generally negative, you may be able to not take it personally. If the other person is acting out of anger or frustration, needing to see themselves as better/smarter, or speaks in a patronizing voice, you are more likely to respond defensively. If it is your child who is being negative, your fears of not being a good enough parent can rise up like a phoenix and prompt a negative response.

One key to becoming less defensive is to recognize imperfection as a normal part of being human. It is also important to learn how to evaluate the criticism and not automatically take it as a valid statement. When you do take something personally, you are giving the other person the power to be right and smarter than you. When you can look at a statement and honestly accept and acknowledge the part that is true and discard the rest, you are on your way to reducing your defensiveness.

Defensive Parenting Scale:

Mother	1	2	3	4	5	6	7	8	9	10
Father	1	2	3	4	5	6	7	8	9	10
Spouse	1	2	3	4	5	6	7	8	9	10
Me	1	2	3	4	5	6	7	8	9	10

THE JEALOUS OR RESENTFUL PARENT

Description:

The Jealous Parent doesn't want her child to have what she didn't have. One of her favorite sayings is, "If it was good enough for me, it's good enough for you." This can apply to material possessions, emotional nurturing, or opportunities to achieve in a career or in life.

The parent lacks a sense of personal or emotional fulfillment. She may want her daughter to feel the same deprivation she felt as a child as a way of bonding. She may simply resent her daughter for having the opportunities she didn't have. It's a painful reminder to the parent of what she missed out on.

The parent attempts to shut out the awareness of her own inadequacies or dissatisfactions. She will have a hard time acknowledging her child's successes and will either ignore, minimize, disparage, or even attempt to derail her accomplishments. Some might even try to take credit by saying, "It's because of what I taught you." Or she might say, "You couldn't have done it without my help."

This type of parent can also try to interfere with her child's friendships and later love interests. She may be negative about her child's friends or romances. She might insert herself into those relationships and try to take over or become a central part of the couple's lives.

Another aspect of the Jealous Parent is her envy of the relationship between the daughter and the other parent. Since the Jealous Parent has significant issues with insecurity or low self-esteem, she will see her daughter's connection with her father as a threat to her own relationship with her spouse. She may resort to criticizing or putting her mate down to her daughter. She may even attempt to limit the contact between her daughter and husband. This can backfire if her daughter comes to her father's defense. The tension and hostility will likely escalate, with unhappy consequences for the marital relationship, as well as the mother/daughter relationship.

In some instances the mother succeeds in forming a close bond with her daughter. The daughter, in an effort to please her mother, will align with her and go along with whatever her mother wants. She may avoid forming close friendships, or will include her mother in most of her activities. The relationship becomes very symbiotic in a dysfunctional way. Boundaries between their individual identities become blurred. The daughter may try to model herself after her mother in a subconscious attempt to boost her mother's self-image. The result is a diminished self-concept for the daughter. Like the planet furthest away from the sun, the father will feel pushed away, left out of the family constellation. A common outcome is both the father/daughter relationship and the marital relationship suffer.

Effects on Child:

Several consequences can occur for the daughter raised under these conditions. She will have issues with her own identity, confusion about what constitutes a healthy relationship, and difficulty forming wholesome relationships on her own. If she does form other friendships or romantic relationships, she risks becoming like her mother, jealous, and resentful. The challenge for her is to develop self-awareness, maturity and self-sufficiency. She will need to distance herself from her mother, which can be painful.

Examples:

I. At a very young age, Annette knew something wasn't right. The subtle awareness started creeping in around age five or six. Her mother Selma, was affectionate, but it didn't feel loving to Annette. She was treated more like a servant than a daughter, under the pretense of being taught life skills. At age five, Selma taught Annette to make her own doctor's appointments and to carry out duties around the house which were beyond her capabilities. Annette was uncomfortable to the point of being frightened. She was unable to talk to her mother, who appeared unaware and unsympathetic. Fortunately for Annette, she had a warm and loving relationship with her father, who was always available to listen. However, he was unwilling to intervene on Annette's behalf and told Annette to "be strong." In an attempt to turn Annette against him, Annette's mother constantly criticized her father. As Annette developed some of her own interests in the arts and writing, her mother was unsupportive and discouraging. Annette caved in to her mother's wishes and demands in order to keep the peace. She did not however, buy into her mother's criticisms of her father—he was Annette's hero and savior.

As Annette grew older, her mother continually criticized her choice of friends; first girlfriends and later, boyfriends. At times she even cut off the friendships Annette was forming. Annette often had dreams of her parents divorcing and going off to live with her father. When she expressed her desire to pursue a college major in journalism, her mother pushed her into teaching. It wasn't until Annette was ready to graduate college that she began to pull away from her mother. Annette couldn't wait to get free of her, and rented an apartment with a friend, using earnings she had saved from various jobs she held since the age of fifteen.

All of Selma's hopes to create her daughter in her own image backfired. Annette's relationship with her mother became increasingly distant, while her relationship with her father became closer. Selma never got the message and continued to minimize Annette's accomplishments while telling her friends her daughter "took after her."

II. Darlene's mother Bess, was much like Selma. However, Darlene reacted quite differently. She became rebellious and spiteful, purposely choosing friends her mother didn't like. This only made her mother angrier, and their relationship became one shouting match after another.

When Darlene was in sixth grade, Bess decided her daughter needed therapy. She sent her to a counseling center. Darlene never realized why she was there. It was a good experience for her because she was able to interact with someone who would listen and be understanding. Bess wanted the therapy to "straighten her daughter out," but that didn't happen. After several months, Darlene stopped going, and there was nothing her mother could do because the therapist supported her daughter's decision.

By the time Darlene was a teenager, she was sneaking out of the house to meet boyfriends. She chose a college major in interior decorating, knowing her mother would give her a very hard time because Bess wanted her daughter to follow a career in the sciences.

As soon as she could, Darlene found a couple of roommates and moved out, taking part-time jobs to cover the rent. Her relationship with her mother never did get back on track. Darlene remained polite to Bess but kept their relationship at arm's length. Bess continued to complain about her "ungrateful" daughter until the end of her life.

Helpful Hints:

Do you have frequent or strong feelings of jealousy or resentment? As with all other Parenting Styles, the key is self-awareness as well as recognition of the effects on your child or even your marriage. See if you can identify the source of your actions, and consider if those motives are genuinely in the best interests of your child. It takes considerable courage to do this.

Observe your child's level of interest in her activities —both the ones you want for her and the ones she wants for herself. Ask yourself: "Is she truly enjoying what she is doing? What are my reasons for encouraging or discouraging my daughter's choices?" These are tough questions that need to be answered honestly.

Do you notice feelings of jealousy, resentment, or frustration because your child isn't doing what you want her to? Are you willing and able to encourage your child to pursue her own dreams when they conflict with your dreams for her? It is easy to rationalize by saying, "I know what's best for her, what will make her happy." "She is too young, doesn't realize it yet, etc." The fact is, no matter how well you know your child, you do not live inside her skin. She has her own unique needs, wants, dreams and desires.

To neutralize any temptations, make a point of noticing the differences in your child rather than the similarities. This applies to her interests as well as to how she reacts to events in her life, and particularly to your "helpful" suggestions. Does she react with passivity, reluctant acceptance, or rebellion? Notice if she acts out in ways you don't understand. For example, she doesn't clean up after herself, forgets to do chores, gets poor grades even though she is responsible and smart. These behaviors may seem unrelated to your relationship, but could be her way of expressing her own frustration and/or rebellion.

Do you have good feelings about your own pursuits and a sense of accomplishment? Can you be satisfied enough? Can you look at your interests through a different lens to make them more rewarding? Can you experiment with other activities? It will be more beneficial to you and your relationship with your daughter when you focus on what you can do for yourself rather than trying to get your needs met through your child.

Jealous or Resentful Parenting Scale:

Mother	1	2	3	4	5	6	7	8	9	10
Father	1	2	3	4	5	6	7	8	9	10
Spouse	1	2	3	4	5	6	7	8	9	10
Me	1	2	3	4	5	6	7	8	9	10

THE COMPETITIVE PARENT

Description:

The Competitive Parent tries to "show her child up" by doing it better. She will often tell her child how good *she* is or was in any given activity. She will usually disguise this as "sharing her experiences" or providing "helpful" information. The parent may be jealous and/or harbor hidden resentments, but attempts to conceal them. Her agenda is to be the "star." The parent continually demonstrates she is the smartest, the best, the most attractive, the most charming. In the most extreme form, it represents the classic narcissistic personality[25]; she is incapable of empathy and sees the world only as a reflection of her.

As with many of the other Parenting Styles, serious insecurity and very low self-esteem are at the root of her behaviors. She sees her child as an obstacle in her constant quest for recognition. She may also want to use her child to bolster her own status. If the daughter does manage to attain success, the mother will try to minimize or ignore her child's achievements or piggy-back onto her accomplishments by claiming credit. For the parent, anything goes in her quest for acknowledgment.

Effects on Child:

Initially, the child may try to compete with her parent in an effort to be heard. She continually strives for attention. She lives with feeling invisible or having little or no value.

If she receives support and healthy acknowledgement from others, she can learn to develop a good sense of self. She might see her parent as an anti-role model—an example of what *not* to do. It may require the child to give up her fantasy of having the loving mother she always longed for. This is a painful process; in effect, she is suffering a loss.

If the child feels sorry for her mother or is overly compassionate, she will continue to allow her parent to take over and still try to please her, even as she becomes an adult. I've seen many women who persist with this pattern right up to the parent's demise. They never give up trying to get their mother's love and validation. They were never able to truly bond with their mother, so they persevere in the hopes of finding a connection with her.

Examples:

I. Florence grew up with a competitive mother. At a young age, it manifested itself in "helpfulness". When Florence would come to her mother with a picture she had drawn, feeling so proud of her accomplishment, her mother Beatrice, would say, "Let me show you some of my drawings so you can learn how to get better."

When Florence was six, her mother suggested they both take dancing lessons. Florence wanted to learn tap dancing, but her mother insisted they both take ballet lessons. Their dance studio put on several performances for the public, and Florence always ended up in the back row while Beatrice had one of the lead roles. Beatrice was on toe shoes while Florence was in ballet slippers, too young and lacking in confidence and interest to progress to toe shoes. She had no desire to compete with her mother.

Her mother always insisted on photos of the two of them at these performances, showing off her "enhanced stature." Florence began to dread the lessons and the performances, but didn't know how to get out of it. When she was twelve, her family moved to a different city and Florence's first reaction was, "Oh good! Now I don't have to take ballet lessons anymore."

Florence's mother never put her down directly—she did it by continually showing how much more accomplished and more attractive she was. When Florence started dating, Beatrice would pay lots of attention to the boyfriends, even to the point of flirting with them in a "casual" way. If the boyfriend was unresponsive, her mother would tell Florence there was something wrong with him.

As an adult, when Florence divorced a man Beatrice thought was smart, rich, and accomplished, her mother didn't talk to Florence for several weeks. She made efforts to maintain a relationship with the ex-husband for several years after, to the exclusion of her daughter. When Florence distanced herself from her mother, Beatrice acted hurt and confused and called Florence an "ungrateful" daughter. Florence managed to find a career she loved and became quite successful. Her determination was fueled in large part by trying to prove herself competent and worthwhile. Of course her mother tried to take credit for Florence's accomplishments. The wedge driven between them was too large to breach.

II Mary Lou's mother Gina, was similar to Florence's mother. Gina's form of competitiveness was expressed by continually bragging about her own accomplishments, showing off at family gatherings to the point of embarrassment for Mary Lou. Gina was also continuously judging her daughter, finding fault with even the most minor incidents.

Mary Lou suffered with bouts of depression and was extremely shy. She was continually fearful that any words she spoke or actions she took would be put down by her mother. If Mary Lou mentioned she liked a particular movie or restaurant, Gina would say, "Oh, that wasn't such a good movie. The one I saw was much better." Or, "X" restaurant has the best food in town. Everyone knows that."

Mary Lou began to retreat from the world more and more. When she was able to move out on her own, she took a small apartment and a clerical job where she would have little contact with people. She lived an isolated life. She saw Gina only when it was absolutely necessary for birthday celebrations and holidays. Even then, she came late and left early, and barely interacted with the guests.

Helpful Hints:

What behaviors and/or reactions do you notice in your child? Is she resistant to your efforts, resulting in arguments? Has she become passive? Does she give in or retreat? These responses from your child can help alert you to something missing in your relationship.

What might be behind your sense of competitiveness with your child? Do you fail to sufficiently appreciate and enjoy your own accomplishments? Do your activities give your life meaning and value? Are there some underlying messages in your own life, perhaps from your parent that prevent you from seeing yourself as good enough? How do you take in compliments when they are given? Do you dismiss them, saying to yourself or others, "It's really not a big deal," or, "She (person giving the compliment) doesn't really know me." "She is just trying to flatter me."

Competitiveness comes from not feeling good enough about yourself. Pay attention on a daily basis to activities that you value. Keep a journal and write down as many of these actions/events as you can. Notice how you minimize your own worth. You may need some external reinforcement and support from someone you trust to erase the negative messages playing continually in your head.

Note: Narcissistic personality disorder is a mental condition in which a person has: an excessive sense of self-importance, an extreme preoccupation with themselves, a lack of empathy for others. The cause of this disorder is unknown. Early life experiences, such as particularly insensitive parenting, are thought to play a role in the development of this disorder.

A person with narcissistic personality disorder may: react to criticism with rage, shame, or humiliation; take advantage of other people to achieve his or her own goals; have excessive feelings of self-importance; exaggerate achievements and talents; have unreasonable expectations of favorable treatment; need constant attention and admiration; disregard the feelings of others, and have little ability to feel empathy[25].

Competitive Parenting Scale:

Mother	1	2	3	4	5	6	7	8	9	10
Father	1	2	3	4	5	6	7	8	9	10
Spouse	1	2	3	4	5	6	7	8	9	10
Me	1	2	3	4	5	6	7	8	9	10

THE USER PARENT

Description:

The child of the User Parent becomes a pawn or tool to use against spouse, parents, other siblings, or even friends. The parent manipulates situations, creating opportunities to show how smart, talented or superior her child is. She will urge her child into activities, ignoring what the child wants. She will push her child to excel so she can say, "Look how smart /successful my child is!" Her goal is to compensate for her own perceived lack of power or credibility.

There are similarities between the Controlling Parent, the Overachieving Parent, and the User Parent, but the motives are different. The Controlling Parent may not necessarily need to prove something to others. Her behavior comes from a need to feel in charge of her life. The Overachieving Parent focuses on her unmet accomplishments or desire for a clone. The motivation of the User Parent is to use her child as a pawn, to make up for her lack of confidence or disappointment in herself. She ignores her own problems, pushing them out of her consciousness. as a way to distance herself from painful feelings.

The following is one example of how this might look: The mother pushes her child into acting, musical performances, sports, or beauty contests. She becomes the very visible "stage mother" attempting to appear supportive and encouraging rather than pushy. You can easily spot her at her child's performances or games. She's the one who is way more excited than her child and is running around trying to draw attention to her child (and herself by association). She finds countless ways to keep herself in the limelight, sometimes to the extent of overshadowing her child.

There are indeed children who have high aspirations to pursue a career, and their parents truly support them. They are passionate about their work, and become successful due to their own efforts. They are not acting out of pressure from their parent. They may even pursue a goal despite lack of support from the parent.

The User Parent is usually the initiator, either subtly or overtly. The child quickly learns that going along with the parent's wishes brings her the attention she enjoys. If she becomes frustrated or loses interest, the parent becomes a cheerleader and does everything she can to keep the child involved. The parent lacks concern with the child's happiness and welfare, or at least it becomes secondary to her own interests.

The difference: a Supportive Parent takes her cues from her child, not the other way around. She closely monitors her child's desires, initiative, and reactions to her parental efforts. If the mother notices reluctance or any other changes in her child's behavior, she will explore those with her and take appropriate action. The child has the freedom to discontinue the activity if that's what she wants.

Effects on Child:

The child of the User Parent quickly learns she needs to please her parent in order to be accepted. She initially focuses on doing whatever will get her parent's approval and love. Being anything other than her parent's instrument of gratification doesn't occur to her.

As she grows older, she will sacrifice her desire to develop her own interests and her own identity. Becoming her own person can even be frightening, as she has had little opportunity to take the necessary developmental steps. At best, the child struggles with pursuing her own emerging talents and interests. She likely will encounter an identity crisis in her late teens or young adulthood.

Examples:

I. Yolanda, from a very early age, was outgoing and expressive. Her mother Esther, was quieter and more introverted while secretly longing to be noticed. From the time Esther was young, she admired and envied friends who were more extroverted. She tried to attach herself to and make friends with those girls, hoping some of it would rub off. It never did, and only ended up making Esther feel more of a "shadow" person. When Yolanda came along, Esther saw her golden opportunity to finally get some of the attention she longed for. She saw Yolanda as a means to show her friends how special she was, and to lose her "shadow" image.

In service of her own needs, Esther read Yolanda's expressiveness as a desire to become an actress. She also interpreted her daughter's outgoing nature as an inborn talent to perform. When Yolanda turned 6, Esther signed her up for dance and drama lessons. She started taking her to auditions for beauty contests, local theater, and any other opportunities she could find for her daughter to be in the spotlight. At first Yolanda thought it was fun, and like most children, saw performing as an exciting and glamorous way to get attention.

As she grew older, Yolanda lost interest in the grueling process of interviews and rejections. Even when she got a role, the time consuming rehearsals and other demands on her life diminished her motivation. She developed a creeping feeling this was more about her mother than her. Besides, she was developing an interest in the social sciences and wanted to pursue her own dreams.

Esther was unable to see how Yolanda's new interest would serve her. She did everything she could to keep her daughter involved in acting, first by cajoling and flattering, and then with demonstrations of hurt, disappointment, and finally anger. Yolanda went back and forth between trying to please her mother and feeling resentful that her mother wouldn't support her interest in the social sciences. They eventually grew apart and Esther became quite depressed. She didn't realize her dreams for Yolanda were a product of her own frustrations and low self-worth.

Once away from her mother, Yolanda was able to clarify her own interests and pursue a career in photography. She found a mate who was supportive and accepting, which helped Yolanda restore confidence in herself.

II. Vera was quiet and shy and loved solitary activities. Her mother LuAnn, resonated with her daughter as she had suffered with shyness growing up. Early on, she got her daughter involved in music lessons, which was okay with Vera, because it was a solitary activity. When her piano teacher suggested she participate in a recital, Vera panicked and refused. LuAnn said, "Of course you will do this, it will be good for you." Vera didn't know how to respond, she was only nine years old. The experience was traumatic for her and she retreated even more. LuAnn continued to push Vera into activities that involved other people, thinking she was "helping" her daughter overcome her shyness and saving her from the misery she had lived with. In reality, LuAnn was trying to use her daughter to overcome her own introversion which of course, didn't work.

Vera became anxious and depressed and finally sought therapy as a young adult. Her ability to function on a daily basis became increasingly difficult. She gradually began to understand the dynamic between her and her mother, and learned to set limits with LuAnn.

LuAnn was upset and continued to press Vera. Their relationship shifted as Vera became stronger and LuAnn retreated from her "pushy" ways. LuAnn also ended up in therapy and they gradually developed a workable relationship.

Helpful Hints:

Pay attention to your own behaviors with your child. Notice to what extent you are pushing her into activities you hope will satisfy your need to prove something or compensate for qualities you lack. Notice your desire to demonstrate your power or intelligence and how you use your child as your proxy.

Take time to recognize and acknowledge your own frustrations, angers, and unmet needs with any given person or with groups of people. Identify the source (e.g. spouse, parents, in-laws, friends, or co-workers). Ask yourself, "What is it about this person or these people that bring out my need to prove something to them?" Then do your best to refrain from acting on that urge. Use journal writing, conversations with a trusted friend, or seek professional help if you are unable to achieve clarity for yourself.

Make it a point to have meaningful dialogues with your child at every stage of her development. Ask her what she enjoys the most, what are her fantasies, what activities make her feel the happiest and most energized. You can start these conversations as early as three or four, adjusting the level of the conversation in keeping with her developmental stage. It may help you recognize the difference between *your* needs you are asking her to fulfill and what *she* wants. Remind yourself regularly that your child is her own separate person, with her own individual needs, desires, and interests.

User Parenting Scale:

Mother	1	2	3	4	5	6	7	8	9	10
Father	1	2	3	4	5	6	7	8	9	10
Spouse	1	2	3	4	5	6	7	8	9	10
Me	1	2	3	4	5	6	7	8	9	10

THE SELF-INVOLVED PARENT

Description:

With the Self-Involved Parent, everything centers around her needs, wishes and interests. While this may occur with other parenting styles, in the Self-Involved Parent the actions are well-defined and more obvious. This is typical of the narcissistic personality[25] (see Note in section on the Competitive Parent), but can also describe a parent who is capable of empathy even while primarily focused on herself.

The difference between the Self-Involved Parent and the Competitive Parent is this Parenting Style will not necessarily include competitive behaviors. The parent's energies will be consumed with trying to get her own needs met and instead of competing with her child, will simply ignore her. She might try to form a bond with her child and sometimes gets involved in her child's life and activities. If there is a conflict between her needs and her child's interests or needs, her own needs will come first. She seeks to carve out a niche for herself, and doesn't recognize the price she pays.

One of the ways the Self-Involved Parent gets what she wants is to form friendships with relatives or friends who are willing to step in and help or even take over whenever she wants to pursue her own interests. She will provide some support for her child, as long as she is getting her own needs met. She can be quite manipulative, both with her children and the substitute care-givers. While attempting to appear like a loving mother and friend she will use whatever means she can to convince her child and the caregiver of her need for time off and may even express appreciation for their help and cooperation. The Self-Involved Parent will spend a major part of her time on herself, and the child will get what's left over, if there is any.

Effects on Child:

A child raised with this Parenting Style will feel disconnected with her parent who doesn't make enough time for her. If there is a bond, it will feel tenuous and not genuine. The child may become self-involved as she learns from her mother. She may become the perpetual pleaser, doing everything she can to get more response from her parent. She may also seek to form strong attachments with the substitute care-givers. In some cases, the child will act out with rebellious or inconsiderate behavior towards the caregivers and/or her mother, as her frustration builds with her mother's inadequate attention.

Examples:

I. Mandy dreamed of becoming a mother, subconsciously seeing it as an opportunity to be totally adored by another human being. She had been raised by a very self-involved mother and feeling deprived, developed an unusually strong longing to be loved and cherished.

When Phyllis was born, Mandy was thrilled and talked about what a great mother she was going to be. She did this as much to convince herself she could be different from her own mother as to assure herself she had learned from her experience.

Phyllis's infancy and early childhood were a dream for Mandy. She felt adored, powerful, and could no wrong. She doted on Phyllis and in turn was idolized by her daughter. As Phyllis started school and began making friends, Mandy had a creeping realization that Phyllis wasn't going to give her everything she needed.

Mandy decided to go back to work and became a party planner where she could exercise her creativity and receive lots of attention and reward for her efforts. She was so absorbed in her work, that Phyllis became peripheral to her life. Occasionally Mandy would try to reconnect with Phyllis by making plans to spend time with her. She would show some initial interest in what Phyllis was doing, but quickly found ways to shift the conversation to herself, leaving her daughter feeling abandoned. After all, Mandy was making a big splash on the local scene, and what she was doing was more important than what her daughter or even her friends were doing.

Phyllis felt betrayed and disposed of. She realized her relationship with her mother was based on a shaky foundation. She went back and forth for a while, alternately trying to engage her mother and ignoring her. Sadly they were never able to establish a solid footing with each other and drifted apart.

II. As an infant and toddler, Danielle loved the attention she received from her mother, Elsa. When she started school and began to form friendships, she noticed a change in her mother. Elsa would discourage the new friends her daughter was making to the point of not allowing Danielle to go to her friend's homes. She did allow the friends to come to their home, using it as an opportunity to insert herself into their conversations and play activities.

Danielle's friends stopped coming over and most of them drifted away, just what Elsa secretly wanted. Danielle was hurt and tried to talk to her mother, but Elsa dismissed her concerns by saying, "She isn't the type of person you want for a friend anyhow." Elsa's lack of self-confidence was exposed in her self-absorbed behavior. She didn't recognize her actions were an expression of her own needs. It didn't occur to her that Danielle's needs were being neglected.

Their relationship became very touchy. Danielle became increasingly angry with her mother, and Elsa responded with hurt feelings saying "You don't understand, I'm just trying to help." Danielle didn't buy this, and started to see her mother for the self-absorbed person she was. She finally began to give up on the relationship. At times, her fantasies of having the kind of mother she wanted would creep in. Danielle tried to tell her mother what she needed from her. Elsa would tearfully agree, but her efforts to repair the damage would last at best for a week or two and she would revert back to her habitual ways.

Danielle eventually sought therapy and with more understanding, her feelings of anger turned into feeling sorry for her mother. She was able to be less angry and nicer to Elsa but still wanted limited and superficial contact.

It was an improved but unacceptable solution for Elsa who periodically tried to maneuver opportunities for them to spend more time together. When she didn't succeed, Elsa would tell Danielle she was ungrateful. She never did acknowledge her own part in doing anything to create the estrangement.

At one point, Elsa told Danielle she wanted to go with her to see her therapist. Danielle agreed, and they had four meetings with a therapist. At each meeting, Elsa was silent, even stoic, while Danielle poured her heart out. When the therapist asked Elsa what she was feeling about her daughter's upset, she shrugged her shoulders and said, "I don't know."

These meetings helped Danielle realize her mother was incapable of empathy. As upsetting as it was, it helped her let go of her fantasies of ever getting what she needed from her mother. Danielle described this process as "the most painful experience I had ever had." The fantasies gave her hope and now she had no hope. Danielle gradually went through a grieving process, the recognition of her loss of not having the kind of mother she needed and wanted. She gradually learned acceptance and as a result was able to be kinder to Elsa. Danielle saw her as the woman who raised her, but not as a mother.

Helpful Hints:

Self-involvement is often a misguided attempt to get some basic emotional needs satisfied. You have a void to fill and have lost faith in finding someone who will be sufficiently empathic and/or supportive. It is like having very strong hunger pains and can only focus on putting food into your body to satisfy the craving. You are unavailable to others due to your consuming need.

The first step is to recognize your efforts aren't producing the results you want. In order to be available to others you will need to find effective ways to fill yourself up emotionally. Spend some time thinking about what you can do to nurture yourself. Some helpful activities include journal writing, meditation, yoga and learning to ask for what you need. Talk to yourself as if you were the most caring, supportive friend you could possibly have. Practice this regularly and it can help you learn how to give the same kind of attention to your child. Consider seeking professional help if your efforts aren't successful.

Self-Involved Parenting Scale:

Mother	1	2	3	4	5	6	7	8	9	10
Father	1	2	3	4	5	6	7	8	9	10
Spouse	1	2	3	4	5	6	7	8	9	10
Me	1	2	3	4	5	6	7	8	9	10

THE MARTYR OR EXCESSIVELY PLEASING PARENT

Description:

The Martyr or Excessively Pleasing Parent sacrifices everything for her child—and everyone else in her life. Her own needs, feelings, and comforts are secondary to the wishes of others. She has very few boundaries for herself and is unable to set clear limits for her child.

Initially, she will impress you with her giving nature and you would like to have her as a friend. After all, there is nothing she won't do for you which is very flattering. She is easy to get along with, always willing to please and go the extra mile. It is difficult not to take advantage of her generosity, and people often do. The Martyr can be outwardly cheerful or she can give the appearance of a long-suffering saint—as this is her lot in life. In either case, inwardly she is someone who doesn't know her value or what she has to offer. She gets her identity from doing for others. She is afraid if she steps out of this role, people will turn away. The impression she often gives is by allowing her to sacrifice herself you are doing her a favor.

Sooner or later, the Martyr runs out of steam and psychic energy. She fantasizes that by giving to others she will get the same back, or at least be adequately appreciated for her efforts. She depends on this illusion to replenish the considerable energy she expends. When the Martyr's energy is exhausted she can become withdrawn, tearful, angry or aggressive. She will often subconsciously resort to making others feel guilty with her suffering looks and comments about how much she has sacrificed. Her formula generally doesn't produce the results she longs for, and she runs out of ideas. The guilt trip is one of her last resorts. If it is successful, she may start using it more often and earlier.

Effects on Child:

The child who is the recipient of the Martyr's behaviors may initially enjoy all the attention and sacrifice her mother is making. However, eventually she will start to feel burdened or resentful, as she recognizes there are too many strings attached to the relationship.

The Martyr may seem to show interest in her child's activities and interests, but the interest lacks authenticity. The parent has a "give to get" mindset. Pleasing her mother becomes important to the daughter as she senses her parent's sacrifice. If she doesn't sufficiently appreciate her mother's efforts, she will pay for it in some way such as a guilt trip or lack of attention. It won't take long for the child to feel depleted and resentful—so much of her energy goes into taking care of her mother's feelings. The Martyr's actions do register with the daughter and have an impact on her, even if she isn't able to articulate the feelings.

As she gets older, the child of a Martyr Parent may adopt the same behavior because she sees how effective it is. She may take on the same role because she doesn't receive enough reinforcement of her own self-worth. She may become demanding, taking advantage of her mother's willingness to sacrifice herself. She might also rebel, becoming aggressive or withdrawn. She is often frustrated in her efforts to have an open and unburdened relationship.

Examples:

I. Lisa grew up with a critical parent. She continually tried to find ways of pleasing her mother in hopes of heading off further criticism. She learned to anticipate what might be coming and took steps to avoid it. Lisa thought this would help. When it didn't, and the criticism occurred in spite of her efforts, she felt there was nothing she could do to save herself. She learned expressing human feelings such as hurt, sadness, disappointment, frustration, or anger were not acceptable. As Lisa grew into adulthood she became the consummate people-pleaser.

When Lisa became a parent, her people-pleasing ways came across initially as very loving. As her daughter Nancy grew older, she started to feel a sense of power over her mother. Nancy began to manipulate Lisa's feelings. She would pout, demand or even fake disappointment or anger. It helped Nancy get her own way. She became the typical "spoiled" child and Lisa was at a loss to figure out how to handle her. Nancy eventually lost respect for her mother. She was frustrated and disappointed that she didn't receive guidance or boundaries and sought out others to supply those needs.

II. Kayla was raised with parents who simply neglected her. They provided little affection, almost no direction, and had a generally benign attitude about their daughter's actions. Kayla constantly tried to please them, hoping to find a way to get some attention. Nothing worked. As time went on, Kayla learned to suppress most of her feelings. When she became a parent, her daughter Judy initially saw Kayla's pleasing behavior as a positive role-model, and adopted her accommodating ways. Their relationship appeared more congenial than the one Kayla had with her parents, but it was based on a façade that didn't allow either of them to be real.

When Judy felt distress, her mother's response was masked with false concern, helpfulness, and affection. Judy's reaction was negative; she didn't trust the insincere words. She eventually grew apart from her mother because as she put it, "I felt like I was living with a shell of a person." Kayla saw her relationship with Judy as an improvement on her own relationship with her parents. She was hurt and confused when Judy backed away.

Helpful Hints:

The Martyr Parent develops this style believing it's the best way to get people to like or love her. She lives with the secret fear that if she were to express herself more honestly, the people she loves and depends on will leave, emotionally and/or physically. Ironically, the pattern of self-sacrifice can be so draining that the martyr may eventually isolate herself. She ends up creating the feeling of abandonment she fears.

Make time to write down what you see as your positive qualities. Ask people you trust for their input on what they find valuable about you, other than your constant willingness to give. Read your list out loud to yourself every day. Continue to add to your list regularly. Pay attention to comments or compliments you receive that are different from being a pleaser. Write those down. On a day when you feel some courage, begin to set some limits and see what happens. Experiment with something relatively safe. Start with small steps as you would when you begin an exercise program. You will need to build some mental muscles and perspective so you can re-learn what your value is to others.

Martyr or Excessively Pleasing Parenting Scale:

Mother	1	2	3	4	5	6	7	8	9	10
Father	1	2	3	4	5	6	7	8	9	10
Spouse	1	2	3	4	5	6	7	8	9	10
Me	1	2	3	4	5	6	7	8	9	10

THE UNEMOTIONAL PARENT

Description:

The Unemotional Parent is unable or unwilling to express feelings and/or affection. Positive feelings and sensitivity to others are especially difficult. Her personality can be outgoing or withdrawn, engaging or distancing. She simply has little or no access to what is going on *inside* herself.

The Unemotional Parent operates much like Virginia Satir's "Computer" personality style[20]. The pattern in her family of origin was to act as if feelings did not exist, so they were never expressed. If anyone did express any emotion, it was dismissed or invalidated. As a result, the child in this family didn't know what to do with her feelings. She learned they were something to be avoided at all costs.

Even if the goal is to avoid only negative feelings, the positive ones will get suppressed as well. You develop the habit of either allowing all emotions or none. You may know people who seem to have only positive feelings. How genuine does this person seem? As humans, we have both positive and negative emotions, and when we are honest and open, both kinds of feelings are expressed. When you are able to recognize and communicate your feelings in an appropriate way, it builds trust—you come across as authentic.

Effects on Child:

The child of the Unemotional Parent learns feelings are not okay. Her parent is not likely to listen to them and will find a way to make them evaporate. She will criticize, minimize or "fix" the feelings by finding immediate solutions. The intention is to say or do anything to make them disappear. The child begins to suppress her own emotions unless she can find a safe outlet through the other parent, friends, teachers or relatives. As she grows into adulthood, she will find it difficult to form a close and comfortable relationship with her mother. She may also need to keep a safe distance with potential mates or other friendships if she fears developing feelings for that person.

Examples:

I There was almost no emotion expressed in Holly's family, either verbally or by actions. Her parents moved through life as thinkers, not feelers. Every experience, every issue, was addressed through a logical filter. As an infant, if Holly cried, her parents tended to her needs in a practical, non-soothing way. She was fed, changed, and put to bed. She learned to be a very obedient child and not to question decisions that were made, no matter how much they affected her.

As Holly grew older, on the few occasions when she came home from school upset about an interaction with another child, her parent's response was to give advice. Her mother might say, "Just ignore it and they will stop." Or, "It's not important, don't be bothered by it. You will figure out how to handle this." She also might respond with, "I'm busy, can't help you with that." Or, "You are just too sensitive—toughen up." Holly soon learned not to bring her concerns and upsets home. She absorbed the message that instructed her not to feel.

By the time she was an adult, Holly had become quite successful in suppressing most of her emotions. When boys came into her life, those with expressive personalities got rejected--she was drawn to boys who were more like her. Her relationships with boys were intellectual, non-romantic, more like friendships. She even chose a mate based on those characteristics.

When her husband left her for another woman, all those hidden feelings bubbled up to the surface, and Holly became overwhelmed, frightened, and on the verge of a breakdown. Fortunately she went into therapy and began to learn about the emotional world inside her. She began to look at her upbringing in a whole new way. Her efforts to educate or reach her parents fell on deaf ears. Holly began to avoid her parents, seeing them only on special occasions. It became intolerable to be around them; she felt her life with them was a desert wasteland.

II Vera's reaction to her detached upbringing was to rebel. Anger and anguish became common responses to the lack of emotional expression in her household. She was desperate to get any kind of reaction from her mother. When her yelling had no effect, she became frustrated and anxious. Vera's school performance suffered, and she had a difficult time forming friendships. Her mother, Frieda, was called to school "conferences" on several occasions to no avail. Frieda was unable to see the connection between her own behavior and her daughter's reactions. She maintained the position that she was doing everything right, and Vera was just a "problem" child.

As Vera grew up, she began taking drugs as a sedative to quiet down the volatile storm that continued to rage inside. She ended up in a drug treatment program, which helped temporarily, but she would relapse within a few months. She cut off all contact with her parents and ended up in a series of relationships with the friends she made in her treatment program. Vera ended up on welfare and was never able to resolve her distress.

Helpful Hints:

If you recognize yourself as unemotional, understand you have built strong walls to deny or suppress your feelings. You may have even convinced yourself you don't have many feelings because they are so inaccessible to you. As humans, feelings are built into our physiology. They exist to help us recognize danger (fear), help fellow humans in distress (sympathy, compassion), worry (an attempt to prepare for bad news), or elation (to help us appreciate the good things). In essence, our emotions are what define us as human.

When you become "unemotional", it is usually because you haven't learned how to manage your feelings. You may have suffered great pain or loss and want to avoid reliving the painful feelings at all costs. There is a Buddhist concept that describes emotions like storms—we can observe them moving in and out, and recognize they are temporary. When you suppress your negative feelings, you also inhibit access to your more positive feelings. Your life will become flat and lose much of its meaning. The key is to learn, or re-learn how to access your feelings, in order to rediscover the meaning and richness of your relationship to others, and to yourself.

The feelings you hold on to or suppress are toxins you have allowed to take up residence in your system. Perhaps you fear you will be too overwhelmed if you let them out. Holding them in is actually more of a threat to your physical and mental health and well-being.

One helpful and safe way to revive your feelings is by journal writing—use your stream of consciousness to follow any thoughts or observations wherever they lead without censoring.

Journal writing is not like keeping a diary. It is taking any event or persistent thought and writing it down. Continue writing whatever comes into your mind, no matter how unimportant or silly it might seem. You might be surprised at what comes up.

Watching movies or listening to music that is sad or from your childhood can also help bring long buried feelings to the surface.

When feelings do start to surface, it might be frightening, like a foreign invader. Many people have expressed the fear if they let their feelings out, there will be no way to manage them. One client expressed it this way: "If I let all my sadness out, I'll never stop crying." She finally did let her feelings out, and she was able to stop. The key is to identify the feeling and decide what you want to do with it, using the principles of Emotional Intelligence.[19] The result will give you a sense of relief and self-empowerment.

If you find yourself resisting these suggestions, or deny your lack of emotion has any negative effect, check with those close to you. Approach family and friends who you notice are comfortable expressing feelings. Ask them how they manage to express their feelings and how it feels to them when you do or don't express yours. It might also be helpful to join a support group where you can observe others expressing feelings in an environment of acceptance and understanding.

Unemotional Parenting Scale:

Mother	1	2	3	4	5	6	7	8	9	10
Father	1	2	3	4	5	6	7	8	9	10
Spouse	1	2	3	4	5	6	7	8	9	10
Me	1	2	3	4	5	6	7	8	9	10

THE IMPULSIVE/EXPRESSIVE PARENT

Description:

In contrast to the Unemotional Parent, the Impulsive/Expressive parent freely expresses negative as well as positive feelings. She has little awareness of, or regard for, the appropriateness or timing of her expression. She can be volatile or effusive, often acting on the impulse of the moment. She lacks a filter, a clearly defined sense of boundaries.

In many instances, the parent does not realize what she is doing. She may truly believe her responses are a legitimate reaction to events. She may have learned to suppress unwanted feelings accumulated since childhood. They build up in her system and when they reach a critical point, they erupt like a volcano. Another source comes from adopting a pattern of response her parents used that ignored moderation when expressing emotion.

Effects on Child:

The child exposed to an Impulsive/Expressive Style will have trouble figuring out how to respond to events. Her parents will either strongly criticize or praise her excessively. At first she will believe what she hears. As she grows older and has exposure to teachers, friends or relatives, she may begin to question her parent's reactions. She becomes confused as she tries to make sense of what is appropriate and what is overblown.

Feeling overwhelmed, withdrawn or anxious by all the drama, she may attempt to head off the strong responses of her parents. She will tend to anticipate a negative reaction and apologize before they can say anything. Playing down her own accomplishments or other behaviors are ways she might minimize over-enthusiastic responses.

The child may attempt to modify what she lived with. As a way of balancing out negative flare-ups she may become highly enthusiastic. In either event, she longs to be noticed, and has learned strong feelings brings her the attention she has been deprived of. It's hard to know what to believe; so much drama is created out of proportion to reality.

The child may learn to adopt the parent's style. As a result, she will have trouble learning appropriate expressions for her own feelings. She may become skilled at mimicking her parent's behavioral responses. She may go to the opposite extreme and develop a passive response to events in an attempt to balance things out. She can also become introverted due to fear of her own strong feelings.

Examples:

I. Tracy became a hyperactive child in response to her parent's drama. The high energy level in the household left little room for quiet times and relaxation. Her father who was not an Impulsive/Expressive. became agitated when his wife was displaying her "high energy" behaviors. He didn't know how to calm her down. He would either yell at her or simply walk away.

Tracy was at a loss to figure out how to react to her parents and to her own emotions. The household became a competitive arena, often creating chaos. Each person was trying to get the spotlight, though none of them realized they were doing this. They were simply reacting to the crisis of the moment, feeling scared, frustrated and helpless. Tracy had no guidance to learn how to feel soothed or subdued. Neither parent knew how to get out of their own way to attend to their daughter.

As she grew older, Tracy's activities funneled into experimenting with drugs and other reckless behavior. This was met with more drama; her parents didn't have a clue as to how to respond to Tracy. Inevitably, it became a new opportunity for her mother to create attention with lots of crying, hand-wringing, and expressions of helplessness. She didn't make any connection between her actions and her daughter's behavior. Tracy's mother did get the attention she craved, but it didn't occur to her *she* needed help, even when well-meaning relatives and friends urged her to seek professional guidance.

Tracy was left high and dry, and continued to pursue unhealthy relationships until she ended up in a mental treatment facility. Even though her parents visited her, there was little or no sense of support or caring for each other. It was a lifetime competition with no winners.

II. Selena's response to her parent's high level of emotional expression was to withdraw into herself. Her parents continually argued, sucking up all the air in the room. While she was intrigued by some of the energy it produced, Selena didn't feel like there was any place for her own feelings to be expressed. She retreated into fantasy, daydreaming and writing poetry in an attempt to find an outlet for her own emotions. Selena also regularly attempted to intervene in her parent's arguments, hoping to bring some peace and quiet into the household. It didn't help.

As she grew older, Selena gave up on the interventions and continued to focus on her poetry. She majored in creative writing in school and became a successful writer. Fortunately for Selena, the chaos in her family led her to a productive outlet and as she matured, the writing became a resource to develop self-awareness and expression. She continued to be withdrawn in social interactions and had difficulty forming close relationships, although she had many casual friends. As an adult, she had minimal contact with her parents, and when she did, she simply became the audience.

Helpful Hints:

If you notice yourself in this style, it may be due to accumulated feelings likely starting in childhood. You might have been raised in an unemotional household, developing a habit of ignoring feelings while they built up inside. This not only creates difficulties in relationships with children, spouses and others, it is not healthy for you. Feelings stockpiled create stress and perpetuate a sense of being out of control. When the pressure inside becomes too great, the emotions spew out. The release opens a floodgate you fear you won't be able to control.

Another source can come from living in a household where expressing strong feelings, both positive and negative, was the norm. You learned to accept this as natural, or at least familiar. You may not have had the opportunity to compete for attention. Now that you are a parent, it's your turn.

You may not be aware you are acting out even when the emotions bubble up. You might see it as honest expression. Or, you may be aware of feelings early on but are afraid to express them. You tell yourself the feelings are not important enough to do anything with them. So you sweep them under the rug, and before long, you have a mound of feelings that has piled up. That's when your feelings become frightening. The accumulation creates pressure inside. What might have started out as a minor irritation can grow into oversize frustration or anger.

The key is to learn to recognize feelings when they are small and find healthy outlets for release. If you aren't aware of your feelings until they build up, get in the habit of checking in with yourself at least once a day by asking yourself:

- "How am I feeling right now?"
- "How is my day going?"
- "Am I noticing reactions from others that I don't understand?
- "Which feelings are okay for me to express and which ones are not okay?"
- "On a scale from 1 – 10, how big does the feeling get before I express it?"

Whether you are aware of feelings when they are small or push them down before they come into your awareness, understand it is easier to deal with feelings when they are minor, they are less scary to you and to others. Think of noticing a small amount of dirt on the floor and sweeping it under the carpet. You won't notice it at first, but as you continue to sweep the dirt under the carpet, a mound will appear until it gets so big you will have trouble going over or around it.

Impulsive/Expressive Parenting Scale:

Mother	1	2	3	4	5	6	7	8	9	10
Father	1	2	3	4	5	6	7	8	9	10
Spouse	1	2	3	4	5	6	7	8	9	10
Me	1	2	3	4	5	6	7	8	9	10

THE INDIRECT PARENT

Description:

The Indirect Parent manipulates, speaks through others, sends unclear messages, or uses non-verbal rather than verbal communication. Her facial expressions, tone of voice, and body language are a primary means of expression. She can be very creative and convincing in her manipulations. Her child gets constant conflicting messages and is never clear about what the true meaning is.

The Indirect Parent may lack awareness about how she feels or what she wants. Or, she may have learned that non-verbal expression is more effective than verbal. She was likely discouraged early in life from speaking up or was the product of critical parents. This can be a form of passive-aggressive behavior. In any event, her non-verbal communication seems a safer means of expressing herself.

When this parent uses verbal messages, they are usually vague because she herself is unclear or fears expressing herself directly. She avoids taking responsibility for her feelings or actions. She relies on more subtle behaviors. Sentences are likely to begin with: "Everyone knows...," "I read an article that says..." or "Your father will be very upset." She may use indirect expressions such as frowning, rolling her eyes, sarcasm, inappropriate laughter, under-the-breath utterances or other body language that reveals her true feelings. When others make attempts to clarify her meaning or intent, she will back off from direct response. She may claim she doesn't know or will turn it around and ask the other person, "What do *you* think I meant?" or, "What do *you* want?" She will deny anything is wrong.

Effects on Child:

The child of the Indirect Parent learns to interpret the indirect communication and acts on her assumption of what it means without checking it out. She takes the chance her response will be incorrect or otherwise misinterpreted. It's not intentional; the child is usually unaware of what she is doing.

She may learn to communicate in the same style as her parent and with others as well, it's the model she learns. If she encounters people who are more direct, she will either be taken aback or welcome the candid message. Noticing others' clear verbal expression could be a learning opportunity. If she does appreciate the forthright way of speaking, she may become more aware of her parent's behavior and make an effort to change things. Perpetuating the Indirect Style will ultimately cause her frustration and confusion. Her communication with others will suffer.

Examples:

I. Trudy's mother was a classic version of Indirect. Since this was the earliest form of interaction she was exposed to, she learned to regularly interpret her mother's messages and to respond in a similar manner. Trudy had no idea there was any other way.

When Trudy started school, she sought out friends who were like her in style, simply because it was familiar. Trudy was well schooled in being indirect as her primary means of communication. When she came across friends, teachers, and other people who challenged her, she got frustrated or simply walked away. Trudy was thrown off guard, not able to figure out how to respond. The lack of clarity began to make her feel frustrated and depleted from constantly trying to interpret even her like-minded friends.

Trudy became depressed and began to isolate herself from others. Her mother, true to form, didn't ask her what was wrong. She fed Trudy articles on isolation and depression and made excuses for her to family friends. Because Trudy couldn't find any source of support or solace from her mother, their relationship became strained and distant. Trudy eventually moved out, lived alone and took a job where she would not have contact with other people. When her mother died, Trudy went into a grieving process that had more to do with a profound sadness for not ever knowing her mother, as opposed to missing her and their relationship.

II. As a young child, Barbara's reaction to the indirect parenting style of both her parents was to throw tantrums out of frustration. Later she tried to compensate by becoming very expressive, much like the Impulsive/Expressive described previously. She would confront her parents regularly and demand more concrete responses from them.

They in turn, repeatedly tried to calm her down, and even sent her into therapy for her "irrational" behavior. Fortunately for Barbara and her parents, she learned to understand what the family dynamic was and the origins of her own behaviors. Barbara was able to become more tolerant of the family atmosphere and sought out friends and other relationships where she could experience a more satisfying interaction.

Helpful Hints:

Indirect communication can initially produce a vague sense of satisfaction or even power, as if you have gotten away with something.

This is usually short-lived or accompanied by other feelings of discomfort, as you begin to feel disconnected with others.

When your verbal and non-verbal expression doesn't match, people will tend to believe the non-verbal expression because it is not as tied to conscious control. An important first step in becoming more authentic is to recognize your indirect behavior pattern. If you have trouble with this, pay attention to responses you get to your non-verbal expressions. Notice how comfortable you are with the reactions which may be verbal (easier to identify) or non-verbal (responses similar to your behavior). Ask yourself, "What in my behavior might be prompting this reaction?"

Keep a journal of incidents describing your behavior and what other ways you could have expressed yourself more directly. Write your thoughts about how the outcome could have been different. This will help you understand what is working, and what is not working.

If you have a friend or relative who will give you honest and kind feedback, ask them how they experience your communication. This is a process of learning how *you* influence the quality of your relationships. Start to experiment with small steps: take one issue that is of relatively minor importance. Make the effort to express yourself directly to someone who you trust. You might need some time to identify the issue and figure out how you would ideally want to express it in a more open and honest way. If you feel hesitant, practice talking out loud by yourself first.

Indirect Parenting Scale:

Mother	1	2	3	4	5	6	7	8	9	10
Father	1	2	3	4	5	6	7	8	9	10
Spouse	1	2	3	4	5	6	7	8	9	10
Me	1	2	3	4	5	6	7	8	9	10

THE ABUSIVE PARENT

Description:

Most parents would not want to see themselves as abusive, so it may be extremely difficult to acknowledge this behavior. Perpetrators of verbal abuse often misuse their authority and prey on those in a subordinate position. Victims of verbal abuse are often told they are to blame for the abuser's behavior and reluctant to take action to end the abuse. Verbal abuse may lead to stress, depression, physical ailments, and other damage.

More often, the spouse or another close friend or relative will be the first to identify the behavior as abusive. However, it may also be problematic for spouses to acknowledge the actions in their mate as abusive.

Recognizing the abuse may trigger a confrontation with the abuser, giving rise to fears of becoming the next victim. It might also force the spouse to reassess the whole relationship and whether it is wise to remain. Sadly, there are far too many instances of spouses turning a deaf ear to the actions of their abusive mate in order to preserve the relationship. The partner of the abuser may feel so much guilt about allowing the abuse to occur, he or she will deny it is happening or rationalize the behavior, unwilling to acknowledge there is any problem.

The Cycle of Abuse[26] describes the process in three stages: the Tension Building Phase, the Accute Battering Phase, and the Honeymoon Phase where the abuser apologizes, tries to make up for it, and promises never to do it again. The person who is battered develops a mind-set called *Learned Helplessness*. These stages apply to anyone being abused.

Unlike the controlling or critical parent, the Abusive Parent inflicts more severe damage. The abuse may be constant and ongoing, or cyclical, but it is *never warranted*. The child lives in constant fear. During the times of abuse, the child may mentally and emotionally remove herself from the actions of her parent in order to tolerate the pain being inflicted.

The mistreatment can take the form of physical, emotional, or mental abuse.[24] Emotional abuse refers to criticizing or denigrating the child's feelings, labeling them stupid, bad, or wrong. Mental abuse refers to being critical of the child's thought processes. Examples of this are: "It's crazy for you to think that," or "Your thinking is bad/wrong/evil. You make no sense at all." Emotional, mental and verbal abuse are terms often used interchangeably. The intent on the part of the abuser is to injure the recipient, even if not consciously. Often the child who has been abused rationalizes the behavior because she needs to see her parent as someone who is capable of taking care of her. She will often tell herself she deserves it.

Effects on Child:

Emotional or mental abuse is more difficult for the child to identify because it is less tangible. A child who has been mentally or emotionally abused will often report that she would have preferred to be physically abused, "At least I would have the scars to show for it." She is confused about what behaviors adequately constitute abuse.

The parent can dish out the abuse in harsh or soft words, or appear to be thoughtful or objective, making it more believable to the child. In any event, the child will initially be puzzled about why she's at fault, especially if she doesn't see anything wrong in what she has said or done.

The child also needs to see her parents as right, as having more knowledge. She depends on them to teach her right from wrong. Often, it's not until well into adulthood that a child will recognize she was abused. Her awareness may be triggered by a clash between another person's reaction to her and her parent's view of her. Or it may come from the child's ability to see her parents more objectively when she is no longer dependent on them for her survival.

The abused child will struggle with her own self-worth. She might develop a fear of others, especially those in positions of authority or who act in an authoritarian manner. These individuals become reminders of her own relationship with her parent. She may be reticent, excessively pleasing, apologetic, or aggressive, all attempts to ward off anticipated abusive behavior. If she is fortunate, in time she will learn to discriminate between justified and unjustified actions. She will learn to stand up for herself or remove herself from harmful situations.

Examples:

I. Devra's father was physically abusive, and her mother was very passive. Her mother's passivity was due to her inability to deal with the father's abuse to her and to her daughter. Devra's brother seemed to escape the father's abuses and his mother's inaction. He turned a blind eye and deaf ear to all of it, going into total denial. He left home at age eighteen, as soon as he was able to support himself and estranged himself from the family.

Devra's mother "disappeared" during the times her husband was abusing her daughter. Devra and her mother quickly suppressed the events and both developed battered women syndrome, becoming helpless[23]. There was no thought of leaving; they didn't think they could make it on their own. They rationalized the treatment as somehow deserved. They were grateful when the father/husband apologized and promised not to do it again. Devra and her mother saw him as strong, and in charge. Ironically, they believed he was creating a safe environment for them. As Devra grew older, she felt the need to take care of her mother and was reluctant to go out on her own fearing her mother couldn't survive without her.

As an adult, after several unsuccessful relationships where she either chose abusive men or extremely passive men, both equally frightening to her, Devra finally sought therapy. Her therapist guided Devra to gradually emerge from her denial. During one meeting, Devra said to her, "You mean when I fell out of my high chair and ended up in the hospital, I didn't really fall out of my high chair?" And, "So, when I fell down the stairs and broke my elbow, it didn't really happen that way?" Devra came back the following week and told her therapist, "I don't know what you did, and I'm really upset. I've had a terrible backache all week and haven't been able to get out of bed."

It was pretty clear that her years of suppression had taken a severe toll on her mental and physical health. Devra became very angry with her mother, more so than with her father. She said, "He couldn't help himself, but my mother could have taken me away from him and saved both of us. She was too weak, and wasn't the mother I needed."

II. In Arlene's family, her mother was emotionally abusive and her father was absent much of the time, spending evenings and weekends working. He was clearly avoiding the unpleasant atmosphere at home and didn't know how to handle it. Work became his escape and justified his denial and masked his feelings of incompetence when it came to dealing with his wife's actions.

Arlene felt confused because she usually didn't understand what she was doing wrong and was thrown off balance by her mother's harsh comments. She felt diminished and never good enough. In order to find some sense of order, she assumed her mother's actions were justified. Arlene believed she was unworthy of her mother's love. She didn't even think about saying anything to her father, her friends, or anyone else. She just accepted her mother's behavior and did everything she could to please her. In reality, it was her mother's own low self-esteem that caused her to be so harsh with Arlene—she tried to make herself feel better by using Arlene as a scapegoat.

As an adult, Arlene decided to volunteer at a battered women's shelter. In her training, she learned what abuse was, and was surprised how she related to many of the symptoms. "I could never justify my feelings because there was no tangible evidence." This was the first step in Arlene's long road to recovery. She eventually came to recognize her own self-worth and went on to develop a healthy marriage. When Arlene became a parent, she went back into therapy to receive guidance on how to avoid repeating the patterns she had been exposed to as a child. It was hard work, and it required continual vigilance on her part. The pull to repeat familiar behavior was a strong automatic response.

Helpful Hints:

In order to recognize the signs of abuse you need to acknowledge it is happening. Pay close attention to the warning signs: the three stages of the abuse cycle as described earlier; the behavior of your child, and the behavior of your spouse. It will be helpful to keep a written record of the stages and symptoms. This will make the reality more apparent.

Take note if your child is very fearful, overly apologetic or anticipates negative parental reactions on a regular basis. She may be timid, reluctant to take action or avoid new situations. These behaviors can be attributed to other causes as well, but could be indications the child is experiencing abuse. Pay attention to the child who is very withdrawn or aggressively acting out. You may not be aware of the abuse or be present when it occurs.

If the abuse is emotional, it will be more difficult to recognize. Verbal abuse can be summarized by these criteria—harsh, critical, and unjust, designed to injure.[27] As described earlier, emotional abuse is characterized by guilt trips, denying the child's emotions, telling her she never does things good enough, absence of positive reinforcement, and other demeaning behaviors.

These actions are all a matter of degree. Every parent will have their bad days and bad moments. When those bad moments become regular, ongoing and severe rather than occasional, strong steps need to be taken. However, even if the abuse occurs once every month or two, the child can still be harmed. The critical factors are the degree of severity and lack of justification.

You need to pay close attention to how you determine what is an exception and what is the norm. It can be easy to rationalize your behavior. A once a week or even once a month outburst that becomes physical, screaming, or demeaning can be sufficiently damaging to be considered abusive. The effect on the target of the abuse is an important measure of the seriousness of the behavior. For many parents who are abusive, professional help may be the best answer. It is also important to remove the child from the source of the abuse, no matter how difficult. The roots of abuse run deep, and stories are plentiful of parents who were abused as children and are determined not to repeat the behavior, but still do.

Note: For more information on symptoms and effects of abuse see: references at end of book.[27]

Abusive Parenting Scale:

Mother	1	2	3	4	5	6	7	8	9	10
Father	1	2	3	4	5	6	7	8	9	10
Spouse	1	2	3	4	5	6	7	8	9	10
Me	1	2	3	4	5	6	7	8	9	10

THE OVERINDULGENT PARENT

Description:

The Overindulgent Parent tends to shower her child with clothes, toys, acting or dance lessons--to name a few, that her child may or may not want. She places a strong emphasis on material things as a form of expression of love. She may also indulge her child in a behavioral manner, allowing her to do pretty much what she wants, unable to deny her "pleasures" or "whims." She may not be able to say no, or it may not even occur to her that she needs to say no. She will often rationalize her behavior as an expression of her great love or wanting to give her child what she was deprived of. The parent is either acting out of fear of being rejected by her child or she uses excessive spending as a symbol of self-worth. She doesn't have faith in herself as a parent or a person. As her child gets older, she may try to be her child's pal since she doesn't trust her parenting ability.

Her overindulgence is a symptom of insecurity. She may have been substantially deprived as a child and tries to make up for feeling denied advantages her friends or other people had. Her deprivation could have been emotional and/or material. The emotional deficit is more difficult to recognize since it is less tangible. Material indulgence is often a substitute for the parent's lack of confidence in being able to provide sufficient emotional nurturing.

When the parent isn't able to appreciate her own value she will discount the positive qualities she has even when others tell her. If material or behavioral indulgence was the way love was expressed to her, she may have redefined love in those terms. It was a way of shielding herself from the pain of emotional neglect. Even if the she does know the difference between indulgence and healthy emotional nurturing, she may not have the knowledge, skills, or courage to express genuine affection and attention.

Effects on Child:

The child of an Overindulgent Parent may initially enjoy the benefits, but at some point begins to sense these gestures aren't the kind of love she needs. She subconsciously feels something is wrong, but isn't able to express it. She longs for more authentic evidence of her parent's love.

If the child is unable to get the quality of love she needs from her parent, she may develop other coping mechanisms, such as disinterest or lack of enthusiasm. She might show signs of hopelessness, depression, anxiety or anger. She may rebel against her parent, withdraw, and turn off her emotions. She could grow up to repeat her parent's behavior, adopting over-indulgence as the definition of love.

Examples:

I. Glenda was what many would call a "privileged" child. From a very early age her parents made sure she had the latest toys and the best designer clothes. Her birthday parties were the talk of their circle with expensive entertainment, lots of "gourmet" child food, and elaborate gifts for each child who attended. These parties started with Glenda's first birthday and continued until she left for college. Her first bicycle was designer quality. She was given dance, art, music lessons from top professionals. I could go on, but you get the picture. At first Glenda was excited by all the glitz and the attention it brought her.

As she grew older, Glenda started to feel "out of sync" with her friends---they couldn't afford the display of luxury. And, even if they could, most of their parents chose not to make such a splash. Some of her friends envied her, some of them resented her, and some wanted to get close to her so they could take advantage of all she had to offer. Glenda found it difficult to develop honest and trusting friendships.

Glenda began to resent and reject the "empty" gestures of love and attention from her parents. She went through a difficult period, searching for her own value with her friends. She eventually felt the need to find new friends who would like and accept her for herself. Her relationship with her parents became strained and more distant after several unsuccessful attempts to let them know her values were not the same as theirs.

II. Ginger grew up in a similarly indulgent household. Around age six, she started to throw tantrums, feeling confused about what was missing in her emotional life. She had no role models to help her understand the source of her angst. Gradually she learned to define love as material indulgence and carried that perspective into her adult life. When she became a parent, she had strong feelings for her child, but didn't know how to express them, so she simply repeated the pattern she had learned.

III Peggy came from a family who struggled financially. They were so consumed with trying to make a living, they paid little attention to Peggy's needs. Her parents were also emotionally unexpressive. As she grew up, Peggy assumed her parents' lack of emotional expression was due to the financial stress. She decided when she became a parent, she would make sure her child had all the material advantages. By doing this, she believed her child would not suffer the deprivation she had. Peggy was unable to make the distinction between emotional fulfillment and material compensation.

Helpful Hints:

Take some time to review your own upbringing. In what ways were you nourished or rewarded? Do you recall feelings of being deprived or overindulged? Feeling materially or emotionally deprived can motivate you to compensate for not getting your needs met. If you were overindulged as a child and it was the main way you were validated or was a substitute for showing love and attention, you may not have learned to express caring in other ways.

Think about the most significant ways you feel or would like to feel validated and loved today. What do others do or say to help you feel better about yourself as a person? What makes you feel truly understood and accepted for who you are?

Have a conversation with your child if she is old enough—age four is an appropriate age to start a dialogue. At younger ages your child will not have the cognitive development to comprehend the verbal concepts. Under age four the validation should be more behavioral. It should include lots of hugging, eye contact, participating in play activities and encouraging your child to share. When your child is old enough to have the ability to express herself, ask her, "What kinds of things make you feel really good inside?" You can also ask, "What makes you *feel* loved? Each child will be different, and it's important to find out what gives *your* child a sense of being valued.

This quote from Maya Angelou sends an important message: "I've learned that people will forget what you said, people will forget what you did, but people will never forget how you made them feel."[28]

Overindulgent Parenting Scale

Mother	1	2	3	4	5	6	7	8	9	10
Father	1	2	3	4	5	6	7	8	9	10
Spouse	1	2	3	4	5	6	7	8	9	10
Me	1	2	3	4	5	6	7	8	9	10

THE LAISSEZ-FAIRE PARENT

Description:

In direct contrast to the Smothering Parent, the Laissez-Faire Parent has a hands-off approach to her child. She doesn't set any limits or provide direction to her child's activities or actions. She seems not to care at all about her child. She shows little or no interest to the point of appearing not to want her child around. She doesn't express emotion, affection, or feelings. Unlike the Unemotional Parent who may show interest, this parent reveals nothing as if she is an empty shell.

The Laissez-Faire parent may not have wanted children in the first place. She may feel deeply inadequate as a parent and rather than make mistakes, takes a hands-off approach. She may be the offspring of a Smothering or Over-Controlling Parent and overcompensates by going to the opposite extreme. She may also have experienced such severe emotional turmoil in her family of origin that she is determined to avoid doing anything in order not to rock the boat.

This parent may in fact care a great deal but has adopted a philosophy of being a hands-off parent, determined to "teach" her children by forcing them to figure things out on their own. She might even rationalize her actions as a desirable way of parenting, maintaining it is a way to "help" her children become self-sufficient.

Effects on Child:

The child of the Laissez-Faire parent suffers from a lack of direction, absence of boundaries and limits, and little or no emotional contact. At times she will long for a display of emotion, even if it is negative. Her world feels empty.

This can be pretty frightening to the child. She may make attempts to get some reaction out of her parent by acting out to a moderate or extreme degree. She may compensate in a positive way by becoming a high achiever. Her actions turn negative if she turns to drugs or alcohol, smokes, becomes promiscuous or develops behavior problems at school. Whatever ways she shows it, it's a desperate attempt to get attention from her parent.

Even though the parent may love her, the child won't have any tangible experience of feeling loved. There may be times when she enjoys the lack of restrictions and will take advantage by experimenting with behaviors to test her freedom. While she may not be conscious of her motives, her conduct is in fact designed to force her parent (or someone) to set some boundaries. She can also become very angry out of frustration when she gets no sign of love or limits from her parent.

Examples:

I. Lila was the product of a controlling father and an over-protective mother. She grew up feeling she had no room to breathe or to think for herself and was fearful of expressing any ideas, opinions, or emotions. She knew they would either be shot down or smoothed over.

When her daughter Cindy came along, Lila was determined not to impose either of her own parent's examples on her child. As a result, Cindy never received any feedback on her behavior, guidance on life, or limits on her actions. In an effort to get some direction, she begged for input and was met with, "Do what you think is right." How could Cindy know what was right, except by what she learned from TV shows and her friends?

By the time Cindy became a teenager, she was learning to like her "freedom," especially when her friends would say, "My parents won't let me do that." It was kind of fun, even though deep inside she was still scared. Cindy began experimenting with drugs, sex, and other risky behaviors. She became a discipline problem in school, and her teachers needed to come down hard on her. She spent a lot of time in the principal's office and more than once her parents were called in for a conference. Lila was the one who usually showed up and maintained her position of raising her daughter to think for herself. She rationalized the purpose of her daughter's behavior as typical "growing pains."

When Cindy graduated high school by the skin of her teeth, she took a job as a waitress, found a roommate and moved out. She had minimal contact with her parents. At her job she found a mentor in one of the older waitresses, who encouraged her to get counseling. She resisted at first. After several failed relationships Cindy had nowhere else to turn and finally sought help from a therapist. Fortunately, after several months in therapy, she learned how her mother's philosophy had impacted her choices in life. She gradually began to turn herself around. She never did stop longing for some expression of love from her mother.

II. Wendy was the daughter of a Laissez-Faire mother and unlike Cindy, she saw her mother's lack of direction as an opportunity to take charge. She started to run the household, made many decisions and even told her mother what to do. Because her mother, Nadine had no confidence in herself, Wendy's actions came as a relief to her.

In fact, Wendy continually tested her mother's responses to see where Nadine might set limits. She never did. Wendy responded by becoming more aggressive, to the point of making strong demands and at times was verbally abusive. Wendy was not only abusive to her mother, she treated other authority figures in her life in the same way. She was desperately seeking healthy and appropriate direction and guidance. At school she found direction in the form of visits to the principal's office and being labeled as a problem child. Since Nadine never stepped in, Wendy ended up going from one school to another, never figuring out the cause and effect relationship of her actions. She was desperate to find someone to set healthy limits.

Finally, at the fourth school, she found a teacher who recognized what Wendy needed and was able to show some empathy and set some limits. This was a turning point in Wendy's life, and she slowly began to form healthier relationships. She did continue to struggle with her demanding ways and at times lost her bearings. Wendy was eventually able to marry a man who understood her struggles and while there were many rocky times, the marriage survived.

Helpful Hints:

If you think this describes you, even in moderation, pay attention to how your behavior is affecting your child. Often children will respond to the lack of attention by rebelling or by trying to become the "perfect" child.

If you notice these behaviors in your child, begin experimenting with different ways of responding to her. Make it a point to show more interest in her schoolwork or other activities she pursues. Pick situations where your interest is genuine. You can develop a more genuine interest by talking to your child about what the activity means to her. This may require you to be well-rested and free of other preoccupations. Learning to focus through practices like Mindfulness Meditation[14] can be a helpful way to clear your mind. When you are able to achieve some clarity, notice your child's response to your changed behavior and/or attitude.

You might not see much difference at the beginning because your child may be surprised at the change she sees in you and not trust it. She may even test you by challenging or ignoring you, or she may act out in some other way.

If you are able, begin to have dialogues with your child about how she is feeling about her relationship with you. Make sure you are asking open-ended questions that can't be answered with "yes" or "no." (Read the information on Communication Skills in the Appendix). Focus on listening, and do not attempt to explain or justify your actions in any way. Notice what feelings come up for you. You may have a lot bottled up inside that is creating a barrier, keeping you from connecting with your child. If you have difficulty listening and attending to your child, your other options are to regularly keep a journal using stream of consciousness writing or to seek the guidance of a therapist.

Laissez-Faire Parenting Scale:

Mother	1	2	3	4	5	6	7	8	9	10
Father	1	2	3	4	5	6	7	8	9	10
Spouse	1	2	3	4	5	6	7	8	9	10
Me	1	2	3	4	5	6	7	8	9	10

THE COOPERATIVE/COLLABORATIVE PARENT

Description:

The Cooperative/Collaborative Parent treats her child with respect and provides her with opportunities to participate in decision-making where appropriate. The parent pays attention to how much ability and maturity her child has at any given age. She recognizes what is an acceptable level of responsibility and what would be overwhelming to the child. She gives her child credit for having good sense, sound instincts, and the capability to act in a responsible way. Her actions are consistent with the child's developmental stage. The theme is, "Do nothing regularly for your child that she can do for herself."

The parent learns to strike a healthy balance between doing too much or too little. She is frequently supportive by showing genuine interest and encouragement without taking over. She achieves this with appropriate physical and emotional distance. She will avoid "hovering" and allow her child to feel her own sense of space and individuation.

The challenge is to primarily exert your authority *only* when you objectively see your child's decisions as actually having the potential for tangible harm to herself. The following behaviors need to be addressed quickly and assertively: your child becomes a bully at school, she spends time on risky internet sites, or she dresses seductively at a young age. There are also other behaviors you want to attend to: unhealthy eating habits such as very little or way too much; habits such as cutting herself, pulling hair out or other behaviors that are physically damaging. These practices indicate a need to seek professional help.

The way you as the parent define "harm" can be subjective. If your child decides to go to a trade school instead of a traditional four or five year university, you could see this as "harmful" to your child. If she wants to become an actor, artist, or musician, you may see this as "risky" because you see the struggles ahead that accompany the pursuit of these types of careers.

These are harmful behaviors *in the parent's eyes*. Your perception of "harm" as the parent has more to do with the values you have adopted, perhaps even arbitrarily. Your perception of "harm" can result from giving too much credibility to opinions from "authority" figures. Those "authorities" can be parents, relatives, friends, religious leaders, teachers, or the media. You may define the behavior as "harmful" when you see it as going against your wishes or dreams for your child. This is a very different situation than the child who as a teenager, decides to take up smoking, drinking, drives without seatbelts, or engages in risky sexual behavior.

Effects on Child:

When you practice this style effectively you will see your child develop self-confidence and self-sufficiency as she grows. She will also become more resilient, able to bounce back after upsets and disappointments. She will be more willing to express feelings and come to you with problems and concerns in her life. The communication will be open and honest and there will be a level of trust between you and your child. Each of you will feel a comfort level with the other.

Examples:

I. Earlene spent a lot of time reading about parenting. She gravitated towards books with the theme of raising a self-sufficient child. She was working full time at a very demanding job, and without realizing it, was looking for a way to make her job as a mother less demanding.

Earlene had learned about collaboration through her job and saw how she could apply it to her parenting. She encouraged her daughter, Felice to make decisions early on and was supportive and offered appropriate guidance.

As soon as Felice seemed ready, Earlene turned over more and more responsibility to her. She was proud of the way her daughter was able to manage on her own. Earlene felt relieved and started backing off her involvement with Felice. She thought she had created a collaborative model in her parenting.

What she failed to notice was Felice's disappointment in the diminished interaction she had with her mother. Even though Felice was capable and competent, she still longed for support and connection with her mother. Her competency was not a substitute for sharing and feedback. Felice did talk to her mother about this and was able to express herself clearly about her emotional needs. Initially, Earlene was taken aback. She had to come to terms with her own agenda that hadn't allowed for her daughter's sensitivities. Because she was committed to her parenting, she learned to make adjustments in her time and priorities. It took some time and hard work, but the relationship between Earlene and Felice got back on track.

II. Denise learned about this parenting model from a seminar she attended. She decided it would be her preferred parenting style once she became a parent.

When her daughter Therese was born, Denise was surprised at the overwhelming feelings of love, responsibility, and protection that came over her. When these emotions tempted her to become more authoritative and over-protective, she went through an internal struggle to maintain and stay true to her original goals. At times her over-protective instincts prevailed, and at other times her authoritative impulses won out.

Fortunately, Denise was very committed to her belief in the value of the cooperative/collaborative style as the healthiest and most positive path for Therese. She was able to sit back and reflect on those instances where she fell prey to her other impulses. In doing so, Denise learned some valuable lessons about herself. She was able to observe how Therese responded when she "fell off the wagon" and noticed the effects of different behaviors on her part. The result was not only beneficial to Therese, it was a learning and growing experience for Denise. She learned to respect herself more and this became added reinforcement to implement her parenting goals.

Therese of course was the beneficiary. She grew up with a sense of self-confidence, an ability to make mistakes and learn from them, and to trust in herself. There were times when she just wanted her mother to tell her what to do and tried to convince Denise that was what she needed. Denise noticed and listened. When she was up to her game (which was *not* 100% of the time), she was able to help her daughter identify the feelings she was having and help her work through them. Therese grew up feeling heard, understood, supported, and got the message her mother had great confidence in her ability to figure things out. As a result, Therese developed a healthy self-image.

Helpful Hints:

One way to foster a healthy balance is to engage your child in the decision-making process whenever suitable. The type of discussion, your child's age, and the individual personality of your child are all factors to consider. Give considerable thought to your child's stage of development and guide your discussion accordingly. For a younger child, ages around four to eight, use the decision-making process on simple or relatively unimportant issues. This will help her to prepare for the more important issues that will come up as she gets older.

If it is appropriate, ask her what thoughts or ideas she has about the subject at hand. Ask her to talk about the pros and cons of any potential decision. Give her the time to express herself fully *before* inserting any of your own thoughts or ideas. This gives her the opportunity to recognize and use her own internal resources. The next step is to ask her to evaluate each of her ideas and identify which ones would be preferable and why. Your biggest challenge is to refrain from jumping in too quickly. The purpose is to allow your child to develop her own abilities in decision-making. This process takes more time and thought and requires restraint on your part to "share" the wisdom of what you have learned.

If your child is truly stuck and can't come up with any ideas or comes up with only one or two, you can engage in brainstorming, where each of you contributes ideas, including spontaneous or illogical ones. You can make it a playful experience. Make sure you do not censor or evaluate any ideas, simply write them all down. Once a substantial list has been generated, ask your child to evaluate each option and narrow down the list. Again, you refrain from offering opinions as difficult as it might be to contain yourself.

Once your child has made her decision, she can be *guided* as how to implement it. Notice: "guided," not "told" or "given ideas." Ask open-ended questions such as "How will you go about doing this?" or "What ideas do you have?" and then, "How do you think that will work?" Avoid questions that only require a *Yes* or *No* answer or questions that begin with the word, "Why?" When you ask a "Why" question, it can put your child on the defensive because she may feel she needs to justify or explain, and she can hear it as disapproval or criticism.

Even with these questions, you need to pay attention to your non-verbal actions. Tone of voice, facial expression, and body posture can convey a strong message of approval or disapproval. As a parent, it's important to observe your own feelings about the process itself and the responses you receive from your child. You need to make up your mind before beginning that you truly value this course of action and are willing to facilitate your child's growth in this way. You also need to be able and ready to support her in the choices she makes, as long as you can objectively agree they are appropriate for her even if you might make different choices. Your emotional expression of encouragement and support are essential components of this approach.

If the child does not make suitable decisions (age appropriate, ethical and achievable), then you do need to step in and ask her to reevaluate. In some cases you will need to assert your authority as a parent and set limits, always in a thoughtful, clear and considerate manner.

While this is a healthy and positive parenting style, there can still be individual differences in how a child will react. It may produce positive effects or you may find your child is challenging you. Testing is a normal part of the growth process and doesn't necessarily mean your parenting skills are lacking. Each child who comes into the world brings with her genetic predispositions to temperament. To what extent genes impact temperament is a continual subject of debate and research. It is important to allow for individual differences. It's also important not to make excuses for behaviors that are not acceptable in your child and yourself.

Make it a regular practice to observe yourself, your child, and your relationship without obsessing about it. If and when you notice behaviors in your child that concern you, take the time to learn what the source might be. Ask yourself (or your child) if there is anything you are doing that might be prompting her actions. It is also a good time to have a dialogue with your child about what could be going on in her life that concerns her. In addition, pay attention to your child's developmental stage, and how much of her behavior can be attributed to her growth challenges.

Cooperative/Collaborative Parenting Scale:

Mother	1	2	3	4	5	6	7	8	9	10
Father	1	2	3	4	5	6	7	8	9	10
Spouse	1	2	3	4	5	6	7	8	9	10
Me	1	2	3	4	5	6	7	8	9	10

THE CHALLENGE

It is a real challenge for you to discriminate between your own needs and your genuine desire to be helpful to your child. The lines get blurred early on, during those early stages of bonding with your child. How can you maintain the bond in appropriate ways as your child grows and matures? How can you distinguish between your need to preserve the bond without depriving your child of healthy development and the formation of her own identity?

If you have read this far, the assumption is that you really are committed to cultivate and nurture a healthy and positive connection with your child. This means you read through each Parenting Style and are able to be honest in identifying what your contributions are, both positive and negative, in the evolution of your relationship. To take your share of the responsibility, *no more, no less*, is key to creating the most beneficial model for your child and to become more authentic for yourself.

A lot of your ability to succeed depends on how well you as a parent have learned to deal with loss and letting go.

The experience of parenting is a series of gains and losses: you gain an infant and lose your freedom; you gain a toddler and lose the infant; you gain the child and lose the toddler; you gain the teenager and lose the child; you gain the adult and lose the teen. And, when your child is fully grown, you begin the process of letting go of your attachment to being a *parent*.

As stated earlier, *you will always be a mother, but when your child becomes an adult, your role as a parent is pretty much done.* You can continue to be caring and supportive as you let go of your impulse to control. Recognize your attraction to the influence you had when your job was to guide your child into maturity. Your adult child may continue to come to you for advice. Resist the temptation to tell her what to do. Instead, ask her what she thinks are options for her. Do everything you can to encourage her to come up with her own solutions while being caring and supportive. This will show her you trust her. It will help her feel more confident and willing to take responsibility for her own life.

If you've done your job well, you can be reassured that you have helped your child become a competent and high functioning member of society. After all, isn't that what you truly want?

SUMMARY PROFILE OF PARENTING STYLES RATINGS

The purpose of the section on Parenting Styles is to help you identify your predominant styles and to provide a starting point to better understand your relationship with your child. It's an opportunity to think about changes you might want to make. You might want to consider having a dialogue with your child if she is old enough and mature enough to engage in an objective discussion. You can begin to experiment with your own behaviors and observe what the effects are on your child and your relationship with her. You might be able to make changes on your own, or you may consider enlisting the help of a professional.

Directions: Enter the number rating you listed **for yourself** *with each parenting style. This chart should help you to see more clearly where your parenting styles intersect, overlap, or don't show up at all. When you complete this chart, it will provide some guidance for you to figure out your next steps.*

	Critical	Over-Protective/ Smothering	Nurturing	Over-Achieving	Helpless/ Dependent
1					
2					
3					
4					
5					
6					
7					
8					
9					
10					

	Controlling	Encouraging	Defensive	Jealous/ Resentful	Competitive
1					
2					
3					
4					
5					
6					
7					
8					
9					
10					

	User	Self-Involved	Martyr	Unemotional	Impulsive
1					
2					
3					
4					
5					
6					
7					
8					
9					
10					

	Indirect	Abusive	Indulgent	Laissez Faire	Collaborative
1					
2					
3					
4					
5					
6					
7					
8					
9					
10					

APPENDIX

The following articles and questionnaires are designed to provide additional Information, assessment, and suggestions for further reflection. These exercises will also help your journey towards a more whole and healthy relationship, both with your child and yourself. It will be helpful to review the sections in the book that apply to each of these topics.

A. Helping Your Child Identify Feelings

B. The Magic of Listening

C. Learning from Your Children

D. Effective Communication

E. Healing Relationships

F. Children Learn What They Live

G. Controlling your Environment

H.-1 Developing an Internal Sense of Control

H.-2 Developing an Internal Sense of Control-Assessment

Appendix A:

HELPING YOUR CHILD IDENTIFY FEELINGS

How often has your child run to you upset, saying "Tommy pushed me down," or "I caught Cindy cheating, and now she won't talk to me," or, "I was the only person not invited to Polly's party." Can you think of what your typical response is/was? If you are like many parents, it will be some version of, "You poor thing," "That's awful, just don't have anything to do with him/her," or, "I'm going to tell her parents about this."

A lot of parents, in their desire to ease their child's pain, quickly jump in and try to fix the distress by soothing, giving advice, or blaming the injuring party as a show of support. Some of this comes from the parent's discomfort when her child is upset. These responses are intended to help the child get past the hurt and help the parent get past her own pain over her child's distress. It is a knee-jerk reaction to feelings that bubble up in your child and/or you. I have worked with many parents who understand this and still can't seem to find a more effective way to respond to their child due to their own high level of anxiety, worry, or fear.

To tolerate the discomfort when you put your own feelings aside for the benefit of your child requires practice, reinforcement, and awareness. You need to regularly listen *first*. Allow your child to have sufficient opportunity to release her pent-up feelings before you move on to find ways to resolve the issue.

When a parent attempts to soothe or problem-solve too quickly, the child doesn't have the opportunity to ease the tension she is experiencing. It denies her the opportunity to learn more about herself and her own feelings. It can also lead to a build-up of stress in the child that can result in depression, acting out, and even physical illness. When you take the time to listen, she experiences relief and emotional clearance. It gives her the opportunity to develop an internal sense of control and builds self-confidence.

You can establish the habit of helping your child learn about her feelings as soon as she begins to understand your words, around the age of two or earlier. At this stage, your most appropriate parental response is to comfort her, as she is too young to do much problem solving. Along with soothing, you can help her find words to describe her feelings. "You must be feeling sad/scared/hurt "(choose one) is one example. Then give her time to take in and digest what you've said. You will create safety and an opportunity for her to discover names for what she is experiencing. She will learn how to identify and express feelings as she grows. This is one of the building blocks to taking charge of her life.

When she doesn't understand her feelings, she lives with an unknown enemy: the distress she is experiencing. Naming feelings is the first step in her discovery of ways to manage her internal life. The reason the soothing behavior alone is not sufficient is the child can get the message you are trying to make her feelings go away or it's not okay for her to have unpleasant feelings. By helping her identify and express her emotions, you let her know her feelings are natural and acceptable, even if uncomfortable

As your child gets a little older, she will become better at expressing her feelings. When she comes to you upset about something, your first response might be, "Tell me more." And then, "How did that make you feel?" or, "Tell me how that feels to you." It's important for her to focus on her experience and how it affects her. You can also remain silent and communicate by body language your interest in hearing more or simply saying, "And then what happened?" Use the cues you get from your child to figure out how to respond.

In your efforts to help, recognize that some children will be visibly upset and want to run off to their room to sulk, cry, or scream. It's wise to respect whatever way she needs to deal with her feelings at any given time. If she does run off, just say, "I'm here whenever you decide you want to tell me more or share your feelings with me." It's not helpful to try to pull feelings out of her when she's not ready to share them with you. It's also not helpful to try to hold her and comfort her unless she indicates verbally or non-verbally that's what she wants. When you pay close attention to her non-verbal behavior you will likely learn what to do—or not to do.

Keep in mind each child is different and will have different needs regarding how she wants you to be with her. When you pay attention to her subtle or not so subtle signs you will get the best information possible on what will be most helpful to her.

It surprised me the first time my daughter, at age twelve, told me she didn't want to be held and comforted. She said, "It feels like you are trying to keep me from having my feelings. I need to be upset for a while." Another child might react in just the opposite way, feeling uncared for unless you put your arms around her. It's best to avoid saying,

"Everything will be okay," a common phrase that may or may not be true. It is more helpful to say, "You are really upset now. This will pass. When you are ready, we can talk about how you are feeling and figure out some ways to manage situations like this."

Appendix B:

THE MAGIC OF LISTENING

Here's the challenge: When your child needs you to, are you willing to fully enter into her world, and to suspend your own ego needs, wishes, preoccupation with your life, your values and your agendas for the moment? Can you be with her where she is, and view the world through her lens, her perspective?

When you are willing and able to do this, something magical happens, and each of you benefits. Your child will experience being fully seen and heard, her very existence will be validated. You will, for that time, liberate yourself from the constraints of your own self-imposed limitations. As you develop the habit of listening, you will gain a new appreciation for who your child is and who you are. You and your child will be able to connect in a way some people never get to experience in their lifetime. Each of you in those moments can be fully whole, fully authentic, and free. There is no better bonding experience than this. And it just might be life-changing. It will be those moments you will hold dear, that you can carry with you always and will sustain you in times of stress.

It is similar to the experience of being in "flow." Can you think of a time when you were completely absorbed in an activity where time fell away, where no distractions, no demands, internal or external, could reach you. It might have been a moment in nature, when you were engaged in a creative activity, when you were deep into a meaningful and heartfelt dialogue with someone, when listening to beautiful music, or when reading a book that captured your mind, your heart, your soul. It requires letting go of judgment, evaluation, and perfectionism. Ironically the outcome of being in this flow state will produce the best possible outcomes; born of creativity, clarity, and freedom.

In today's world, when we are being pulled in so many directions, continually responding to real and perceived demands on our time and energies, this experience is rare. In addition, our attachment or addiction to our "devices" pulls us away from other people, even as we are texting, tweeting, or on Facebook. We interact with others in a virtual world, in a technology connected world with diminished person to person connection. This makes it even more important to recognize and create those special opportunities and make the time to nourish the relationships with people we value.

Note:
1. The concept of "flow"[29] was created by Mihaly Csikszentmihalyi, a professor at Claremont Graduate University and former chair of the Department of Psychology at the University of Chicago. "A flow state ensues when one is engaged in self-controlled, goal-related, meaningful actions. During flow, people typically experience deep enjoyment, creativity, and a total involvement with life."

Appendix C:

LEARNING FROM YOUR CHILDREN

How do you learn to become a parent? You may read articles and books, talk to friends and/or relatives, or attend parenting classes. While these can all be valuable resources, another source of information is equally important and often neglected.

Learning from our children gives you information no outside resource can adequately address: the unique aspects of your child's temperament and personality, as well as specific environmental factors that affect your child's behavior.

Environmental factors include the city or country you live in, your neighborhood and the school your child attends. Other influences are the friends she develops, your family's ethnicity and religious teachings, your socio-economic circumstances, the status of your marital relationship, your own history, value system, and personality. Any of these elements can shape how you parent and how your child reacts to your parenting.

When you pay attention to how these elements affect your child, you will have additional knowledge to help you navigate the path to successful parenting. Your child regularly provides you with clues on how good a job you are doing. Much of this information will be non-verbal, and she may not be aware what her actions reveal. Each time you get into an argument with your child over something you have said, her response will tell you if she doesn't hear it in the way you intended. For whatever reason, it's a signal that she's not able to digest the information. Sometimes her resistance comes in the form of sulking, withdrawing, acting out physically, or tantrums (which can occur at any age). It's unreasonable to expect you can always avoid these situations. You are human, and are subject to your own moods and reactions. The goal is to take advantage of new skills and information whenever you can muster the energy and focus to improve your relationship.

As a child, I recall my father never got angry or punished me. He would sit down and talk to me in a calm voice about whatever transgression I had committed. He asked me what happened, how I felt about it, and what I might have done different. His relaxed composure, without blame or guilt-inducing words had a powerful effect on me, more so than anything else he could have done. He clearly had a unique ability to remain objective and supportive. The strongest message I received was that he cared about me and wanted to help me through a difficult situation. It also spoke to me of his awareness that I did not have the maturity and/or coping skills I needed to resolve the issue in a more constructive way.

While he was a great role model, I can't say I was always able to emulate his unique ability. His style did however, teach me as a parent to listen more and to learn as much as I could from my child about the source of her behavior or feelings. Sometimes my child was forthcoming, sometimes she needed to retreat for a while and then come to me when she was ready. My father's example helped me to take into consideration that timing was important and being on my child's emotional and mental wavelength was very significant. It was far more productive to pay attention to her readiness to talk than to demand she accommodate to my need to relieve my anxiety or insecurity on my schedule.

It is very important to communicate to your child that you care about *her*. Let her know you would like to understand what is going on inside of her. Tell her you want to learn what she needs to discover ways resolve her own internal and external conflicts. One of the most valuable lessons you can provide is to help your child recognize and learn from the consequences of her own actions. One of the most essential skills for you to develop as a parent is the concept of Active Listening[12]. A guideline for that skill follows on the next page.

Appendix D:

EFFECTIVE COMMUNICATION

SENDING CLEAR MESSAGES:

1. _Face your listener._ Maintain good eye contact; give her your full attention.
2. _Keep it simple_. Use language that can be understood by receiver-- at her age level and less likely to be misinterpreted.
3. _Keep your message brief and to the point_. After about 10 minutes, the other person stops listening.
4. _Avoid using clichés_. This makes you sound less sincere and less personal.
5. _Personalize your message_. Use "I" instead of "we," "you," "they," or "everyone."
6. _Take responsibility for your message_. When you want to state an opinion or feeling, don't disguise it by asking a question. (e.g. "I'm uncomfortable with that idea" is preferable to "Do you like that idea?")
7. _Avoid giving advice, lecturing, or patronizing your child._ These messages tend to make her feel inadequate or inferior.
8. _Stay away from using the word "why"_ as in, "Why did you do that?" which prompts a defensive response.
9. _Avoid ordering, directing, or commanding_. This can provoke a defensive reaction.
10. _Communicate respect_. This helps the listener hear you better.
11. _Check to see that_ your verbal and non-verbal messages match.

RECEIVING A MESSAGE:

1. _Listen with concentration_--avoid all distractions, including your mind wandering.
2. _Listen for your child's central message –_what feelings is she trying to express?

3. *Keep your own ideas in the background*—put them on a mental shelf in a closet

4. *Allow your child to express herself fully*--withhold making value judgments or any other comments until she is finished.

5. *See if you can identify with the idea, feelings and attitudes expressed by your child*—put yourself in her shoes.

6. *Notice your emotional reactions and don't allow them to interfere* with hearing what your child is saying.

7. *Ask for clarification of unclear words or ideas*

REPEATING, PARAPHRASING, SUMMARIZING:

1. *Restate the main thoughts, ideas, or principles, your child is expressing in your own words.*

2. *Paraphrase after three or four sentences*--it's easier to handle smaller pieces of information.

3. *Clarify*--Ask your child if your statement is accurate--if not, ask her to restate the message.

4. *Summarize*—in one to three sentences the substance of her communication.
   - *Especially important when conversation is confusing, tense, or emotional for either of you.*
   - *Important in family/group discussions when there is a chance you or others might not understand each other.*

ACKNOWLEDGING:

Your active listening will acknowledge *that you understand the message—this does not mean you have to agree, accept, or approve of what the person has said.* Share your views only after the other person confirms your paraphrase.

> *"It takes courage to stand up for yourself—and to sit down and listen."*

Notes

1. The key is to listen first. When the other person feels heard and understood, it creates an "emotional clearance" that opens up her ability to attend to what you have to say.

2. The skill of reflecting back the meanings and feelings of others (empathic listening). Carl Rogers referred to it as "reflection of feelings." [12]

3. *"It takes courage to stand up for yourself—and to sit down and listen."* –Author Unknown. This quote has been widely attributed to Winston Churchill. According to the Churchill Archives Centre in UK, Churchill did not author this quote and the actual author is unknown.

Appendix E:

HEALING YOUR RELATIONSHIP

1. My Responsibility (write about *only* these topics):

What I Did That Hurt our Relationship:

_____

_____

What I Could Have Done Better:

_____

_____

When you have completed this section, read it to see if you have left anything out, or slipped in anything that are excuses. Revise your responses to correct those items.

2. What might be the source of my Actions – Look at what you have written. Spend some time thinking about where you learned them, or how you came to decide to use those behaviors.

_____

_____

3. From my child's perspective, she saw me as:

_____

_____

I can begin to see her behavior as a way of coping with:

_____

_____

As needing more/less of:

_____

_____

4. What I want to do about the relationship now—If your first response is "nothing," it probably means you are feeling hopeless or defensive or simply discouraged by all the efforts you have made in the past that haven't worked. If this is the case, write down the reset of this sentence: If I knew I could really have a better relationship with my child, I would:

_____

_____

_____

5. Write a letter. This will be a letter to your child that you don't plan on sending. Write down everything you want to say, knowing she will not be reading it. This gives you the opportunity to get it all out and learn more about what you have been holding inside of you.

6. Write a second letter. This will be the letter you plan to send (not an email). Review everything you have written to this point and decide what you want her to know that will likely help the healing. Hint: Taking responsibility, showing empathy for her perspective, and what you have learned are the best chances you have for repair.

7. Seek Help. If you feel stuck, unable to begin this process, or feel helpless or resentful at any point along the way, it is time to seek professional help. If your relationship is seriously damaged and despite these efforts, your child is unwilling to engage in the healing process, it is also time to seek professional help. It is possible your child will not want to go to counseling with you. In any event, it is important that you go, whether or not she is willing to participate.

Appendix F:

CHILDREN LEARN WHAT THEY LIVE

If children live with criticism, they learn to condemn.
If children live with hostility, they learn to fight.
If children live with fear, they learn to be apprehensive.
If children live with pity, they learn to feel sorry for themselves.
If children live with ridicule, they learn to feel shy.
If children live with jealousy, they learn to feel envy.
If children live with shame, they learn to feel guilty.
If children live with encouragement, they learn confidence.
If children live with tolerance, they learn patience.
If children live with praise, they learn appreciation.
If children live with acceptance, they learn to love.
If children live with approval, they learn to like themselves.
If children live with recognition, they learn it is good to have a goal.
If children live with sharing, they learn generosity.
If children live with honesty, they learn truthfulness.
If children live with fairness, they learn justice.
If children live with kindness and consideration, they learn respect.
If children live with security, they learn to have faith in themselves and in those about them.
If children live with friendliness, they learn the world is a nice place in which to live.

Appendix G:

CONTROLLING YOUR ENVIRONMENT

1. What does "control" mean to me?

_____

_____

_____

2. Who are the people in my life I think I have control over?

_____

_____

_____

a)   What do I do to control them (e.g. dictate, manipulate, threaten, compete, etc.)?

_____

_____

_____

b) How well does it work?
Very Well_____ Somewhat_____   Not at all_____

c) What are the reactions from them? (e.g. anger, fear, submission, withdrawal, retaliation):

_____

_____

_____

3. Who are the people in my life I feel have control over me?

_____

_____

_____

a)   How do they control me?

_____

_____

_____

b) I allow it because:

_____

_____

_____

c) The effects I experience are:

_____

_____

_____

4. How much of my time and/or energy is used in trying to figure other people out with the goal of controlling or influencing their behaviors?
A lot_____ Somewhat_____ None_____

5. How much of my time and/or energy is used in planning and implementing my own choices and decisions for my life?

Most of the time_____ Sometimes_____ Little or no time_____

6. In what relationships and/or areas of my life would I like to develop greater control?

_____

_____

_____

7. What steps can I take to make this happen?

_____

_____

_____

Hint: It's all about *you* and what ways *you* can be different with others as well as how *you* can change your perspective and/or attitude.

Writing these answers down will help you clarify the situations and issues that derail you.

Make sure you list the steps you need to take, in order to remedy the situation(s). *Use this as a reminder for you*—keep it someplace prominent and accessible to help you remember.

Appendix H-1:

DEVELOPING AN INTERNAL
SENSE OF CONTROL

The following questionnaires will help you gain a better understanding of how the issue of control impacts your life.

Emotions that indicate you are feeling out of control:

This first checklist is a guide to identifying the symptoms of feeling out of control. You can then use this as a guide to respond to the evaluation that follows.

Circle the number that best describes how often you have these feelings:

	Never				Often
Guilt	1	2	3	4	5
Fear	1	2	3	4	5
Anxiety	1	2	3	4	5
Confusion	1	2	3	4	5
Inadequacy	1	2	3	4	5
Worthlessness	1	2	3	4	5
Worry	1	2	3	4	5
Stupidity	1	2	3	4	5
Helplessness	1	2	3	4	5
Indecisiveness	1	2	3	4	5
Anger	1	2	3	4	5
Frustration	1	2	3	4	5
Jealousy or Envy	1	2	3	4	5
Defensiveness	1	2	3	4	5

Appendix H-2:

DEVELOPING AN INTERNAL
SENSE OF CONTROL-ASSESSMENT

The extent to which you maintain an internal sense of control is directly proportional to your need or desire to control others' actions, words, or even thoughts. Attempting to control others is a substitute for your perceived inability to have an internal sense of control. There is only one person you have any real control over, twenty-four hours a day, seven days a week—*Yourself.*

This checklist will help you understand what is involved in having an internal sense of control

Rate yourself from 1 (never) to 5 (always) on the following items:

	Usually True For Me	Need to Work On
I feel I can handle any situation that arises.	_____	_____
I can survive disappointments.	_____	_____
I am able to function well in times of crisis.	_____	_____
I am open to change.	_____	_____
I am willing to take risks.	_____	_____
I make mistakes and am able to learn from them.	_____	_____
My mistakes do not define me as a failure.	_____	_____
I am able to live mainly in the present.	_____	_____

References:

[1] "On Children" from THE PROPHET by Kahlil Gibran, copyright ©1923 by Kahlil Gibran and renewed 1951 by Administrators C.T.A. of Kahlil Gibran Estate and Mary G Gibran. Used by permission of Alred A. Knopf, an imprint of the Knopf Doubleday Publishing Group, a division of Penguin Random House LLC. All rights reserved. Any third party use of this material, outside of this publication, is prohibited. Interested parties must apply directly to Penguin Random House LLC for permission.

[2] Barker, Eric. *Barking up the Wrong Tree* blog, featured in the New York Times, the Wall Street Journal, Wired Magazine and Time Magazine. 250,000 followers.

[3] Darling, Nancy & Steinberg, Laurence. "Parenting Style as Context: An Integrative Model." *Psychological Bulletin of American Psychological Association* 113:3 (1993): 487-496.

[4] Spera, Christopher. "A review of the Relationship Among Parenting Practices, Parenting Styles, and Adolescent School Achievement," *Educational Psychology Review 17:2 (2005): 125-142.*

[5] Baumrind, Diana. Effects of Authoritative Parental Control on Child Behavior, *Child Development*, 37:4 (1966), 887-907.

[6] Maccoby, E. E., & Martin, J. A. Socialization in the context of the family: Parent–child interaction. In P. H. Mussen & E. M. Hetherington, *Handbook of child psychology: (4): Socialization, personality, and social development (4th ed.).* New York: Wiley, 1983.

[7] Bernstein, D. A. *Essentials of psychology.* Belmont, CA: Wadsworth, 2011.

[8] Erikson, Erik. *Childhood and Society New York:* W.W. Norton & Company, Inc., 1950, 1963.

[9] Leiner, Marie PhD, Ataalla, Mohamed MD, Minding the Child: Mentalization-Based Interventions with Children, Young People, and Their Families in *Journal of Developmental & Behavioral Pediatrics*, 35:5 (2014) book review, 343.

[10] CREDIT LINE: "Figure of Erikson's Stages of Personality Development", from CHILDHOOD AND SOCIETY BY Erik H. Erikson. Copyright 1950, © 1963 by W. W. Norton & Company, Inc., renewed © 1978, 1991 by Erik H. Erikson. Used by permission of W.W. Norton & Company, Inc.
Also: From CHILDHOOD AND SOCIETY by Erik Erikson. Published by Chatto & Windus. Reprinted by permission of The Random House Group Limited, UK.

[11]Siegel, Daniel and Hartzell, Mary *Parenting From the Inside Out. New York:* the Penguin Group, 2013.

[12]Gordon, Thomas. *Parent Effectiveness Training. New York:* Clarkson Potter/Ten Speed/Harmony, 1975 revised 2000.

[13] Merriam-Webster Dictionary, "Unconditional: not conditional or limited : absolute, unqualified <*unconditional* surrender> <*unconditional* love>". Chicago, Il: Encyclopedia Brittanica, © 2014. http://www.britannica.com/ .

[14]Rogers, Carl. *On Becoming a Person: A Therapist's View of Psychotherapy.* London: Constable Publishing, 1961.

[15]Maslow, Abraham H. "Peak Experiences as Acute Identity Experiences". *American Journal of Psychoanalysis,* **21**: 2 (1961): 54–260.

[16] Kabat-Zinn, Jon. *Mindfulness for Beginners: Reclaiming the Present Moment— and Your Life,* Boulder, Co: Sounds True, Inc., 2013.

[17] McGraw-Hill Dictionary, "Pride Goeth Before a Fall," McGraw-Hill Dictionary of American Idioms and Phrasal Verbs. McGraw-Hill Education; 1st edition, New York, 2006. http://www.fisiologia.ufc.br/ABS/McGraw-ill's.Dictionary.of.American.Idioms.and.Phrasal.Verbs.pdf.

[18] Gilles Jr., Robert Paul. "*To Let Go Takes Love.*" reprinted with permission by Robert Paul Gilles Jr. ©1997.

[19] Erikson, Erik. *Identity Youth and Crisis.* New York: W.W. Norton & Company, Inc , 1968.

[20] Lally, Van Jaarsveld, Potts and Wardle. How are Habits Formed: Modeling habit formation in the Real World. John Wiley & Sons, Ltd.: *European Journal of Social Psychology* 40 (6).

[21] Goleman, Daniel. *Emotional Intelligence.* New York: Bantam Books, 1995, 2012.

[22] Satir, Virginia. *The New Peoplemaking.* Palo Alto: Science and Behavior Books, 1988. Use of material: permission granted by Science and Behavior Books.

[23] Merriam-Webster Dictionary: "Symbiosis: biology : the relationship between two different kinds of living things that live together and depend on each other; a relationship between two people or groups that work with and depend on each other." Chicago, Il: Encyclopedia Brittanica, © 2014. http://www.britannica.com/ .

[24] Merriam-Webster Dictionary, "Co-Dependency: a psychological condition or a relationship in which a person is controlled or manipulated by another who is affected with a pathological condition (as an addiction to alcohol or heroin); *broadly* : dependence on the needs of or control by another." Chicago, Il: Encyclopedia Brittanica, © 2014. http://www.britannica.com/ .

[25] Narcissistic Personaltiy Disorder. DSM IV: *Diagnostic and Statistical Manual of Mental Disorders, 4th edition,* 1994, *Washington,* D.C,. American Psychiatric Association, 661

[26] Walker, Lenore. "Dynamics of Domestic Violence - The Cycle of Violence" (n.d.). Retrieved October 23, 2002, from http://www.enddomesticviolence.com/include/content/filehyperlink/holder/The%20Cycle%20of%20Violence.doc

[27] Abuse Symptoms: Mayo Clinic: http://www.mayoclinic.org/diseases-conditions/child-abuse/basics/symptoms/con-20033789. Abuse: Legal Definition: California Courts: The Judicial Branch of California. http://www.courts.ca.gov/1258.htm. The National Domestic Violence Hotline. http://www.thehotline.org/is-this-abuse/.

[28] Angelou, Maya (Author), Buckley, Ronda (Editor).*101 Quotes and Sayings From Maya Angelou.* Publisher: Maya Angelou, 2014. Maya Angelou used with permission by Caged Bird Legacy LLC. www.MayaAngelou.com

[29] Csikszentmihalyi, Mihaly. *Flow: The Psychology of Optimal Experience.* New York: Harper Perennial Modern Classics; 1st edition 2008.

[30] Nolte, Dorothy Law. "Children Learn What they Live*."* Excerpted from the book CHILDREN LEARN WHAT THEY LIVE. Copyright © 1998 by Dorothy Law Nolte and Rachel Harris. The poem, "Children Learn What They Live" Copyright © 1972 by Dorothy Law Nolte. Used by permission of Workman Publishing Co., Inc., New York. All Rights Reserved.

Recommended Additional Reading:

Bradbury, Travis and Greaves, Jean. *Emotional Intelligence 2.0.* San Diego, CA: Talent Smart, 2009.

Bronson, Po and Merryman, Ashley. *Nurture Shock: New Thinking About Children*, New York: Twelve, a division of Hachette Book Group, 2009.

Goleman, Daniel. *Emotional Intelligence.* New York: Bantam Books, 1997, 2012.

Josephson, Michael, Josephson Institute of Ethics, http://josephsoninstitute.org/. Mission: "To improve the ethical quality of society by changing personal and organizational decision making and behavior.

Kabat-Zinn, Jon. *Mindfulness for Beginners: Reclaiming the Present Moment—and Your Life,* Boulder, Co: Sounds True, Inc., 2013.

McBride , Karyl, Ph.D. *Will I Ever Be Good Enough?: Healing the Daughters of Narcissistic Mothers,* New York: Atria Publishing Group, a division of Simon & Schuster, Reprint edition 2009.

Rogers, Carl. The Interpersonal Relationship: The Core of Guidance. In Maslowski, Raymond M., Morgan, Lewis B. (Eds.). MSS Information Corporation. *Interpersonal Growth and Self Actualization in Groups*, 176-189

Siegel, Daniel and Hartzell, Mary. *Parenting From the Inside Out.* New York: The Penguin Group, 2013.

Siegel, Daniel, Bryson, Tina Payne. *The Whole Brain Child.* New York: Bantam Books, 2011.

Siegel, Ronald D. *The Mindfulness Solution: Everyday Practice for Everyday Problems.* New York: The Guilford Press, 2010.

Weinhold, Janae B. and Weinhold, Barry K. *Breaking Free of the Co Dependency Trap.* Novato, CA: New World Library, 2010.

Please Note: All the questionnaires and fill-in forms are available for download on the book's website. If you have any questions, feel free to contact me through my website: www.EmpowerYourRelationship.com.

ABOUT THE AUTHOR

Shelli Chosak. Ph.D. is an expert in human behavior. Her lifelong passion, in addition to her three grown children and five grandchildren, is finding ways to achieve Quality of Life.

She received her Bachelor's degree in Psychology from U.C.L.A., her Master's degree in Clinical Psychology from Pepperdine University, and earned a California state license in Marriage and Family Therapy. She later returned to school and obtained a Ph.D. in Organizational Psychology.

Shelli maintained a psychotherapy practice in Los Angeles for 25 years, specializing in family relationships. During this time She developed and directed a university level two-year certificate program training students to become human services workers in the community. She worked in this capacity for over twelve years.

Shelli served as a consultant to the Los Angeles Superior Court Family Mediation Division (Conciliation Court) for over ten years, and counseled clients referred by the court classified as "difficult cases."

She was a regional coordinator for the California State Task force on Parenting and Families, a member of the California State Senate Judiciary- Family Law Advisory Committee and a delegate to the White House Conference on Families.

Shelli currently lives in San Diego and maintains a coaching and consulting practice.

.

www.ingramcontent.com/pod-product-compliance
Lightning Source LLC
LaVergne TN
LVHW051522080426
835509LV00017B/2166